SOLEDAD PRISON
UNIVERSITY
OF THE POOR

Layout & Design by Peter Troxell

Illustrations by Diana Wright

Typeset by Carol Wolff

Library of Congress Card Number 74-84559

ISBN 0-8314-0038-2

An exchange between students from the University of California at Santa Cruz and prisoners at the Soledad Correctional Training Facility.

Edited by
KARLENE FAITH

SCIENCE AND BEHAVIOR BOOKS, INC.
Palo Alto, California

Dedicated to all members of the Convicted Class and to those who, in the cause of freedom of speech and freedom of thought, are opposed to the jailing of ideas.

"Members of the Convicted Class maintain their constitutional rights of speech, press, religion, and association, and these rights include the free exchange of information, vocally or in writing, and the right to transmit or receive any letters and publications, and the right to assemble with others of one's choosing, including members of the Convicted Class, for purposes of exchanging and debating various viewpoints on the controversial issues of our day."

Article 1, Section X
United Prisoners' Union
Bill of Rights — 1971

THE SOLEDAD–SANTA CRUZ COLLECTIVE

Roberto Arras
Mona Burns
Courtney Cain
Eugene Calhoun
Joaquin Castro
Pedro Chacon
Alma Cota
Ben Dunn
Karlene Faith
Sherwin Forte'
Robbie Freeman
Ruben Gonzales
Ralph Guzman
Phillip Jacobs

Michael Lee
Rebeca Alicia Lopez
William Lute
Francisco Mantua
Theordore Martinez
Stanley Mayabb
Gary Pernell
Ruben Reyna
Richard Risher
Plezena Shack
Arthur Stasney
Deirdre Stone
Debra Walton
Ranko Yamada

TABLE OF CONTENTS

Table of Contents (cont'd.)

FOREWORD

When I first read the prison manuscript I was excited and very troubled by the potential of publishing such a volume. The manuscript seemed almost chaotic in organization, resisting all efforts to impose a structure on it. This chaos ultimately became a virtue. A format emerged which captures that moment in time when students and prisoners met one another. It is the human story of the coming together of many individuals of diverse backgrounds and ways of experiencing life.

This book takes us directly inside the walls of a noted California prison in Soledad. Prison administrators call them "inmates" and, audaciously, "residents"; Karlene Faith's book lets us see they are simply prisoners caught in society's own tumultous creation. We have been led to erroneously understand that prisons "rehabilitate." Literally rehabilitate means "to return to a former capacity." There is no prisoner who wishes to return to the conditions which brought him to the prison.

When Karlene Faith completed her work at Soledad she shifted her attention to the Women's Prison at Corona—the largest women's prison in the country—applying there what she learned from Soledad. Out of this work emerged an extensive educational program wherein prisoners receive college credit for a variety of courses taught within the prison. One hundred and fifty volunteers participate in this program of mutual growth. Calling it a rehabilitation program is, again, misleading; it is a collective with a real sense of sisterhood and purpose.

A second volume is planned that will be composed by autobiographical writings of women prisoners, many of whom have found their voices and speak with the clarity of fresh vision. This new book will also contain excerpts from Karlene's journal showing her personal struggle between working within the prison for reform, and burning down the walls. In the final analysis, it seems Karlene is doing both.

Robert S. Spitzer, M.D.
Editor in Chief

Peter Troxell
Coordinator

SCIENCE AND BEHAVIOR BOOKS, INC.

PREFACE AND ACKNOWLEDGEMENTS

During the spring of 1971 a group of students from the University of California at Santa Cruz met with a group of prisoners once a week for two months at Soledad Prison, and the writings that emerged from these meetings form the basis of this book. Everyone in the combined group had agreed that we should publish a record of our experience. Inspired by the collective enthusiasm and goaded by my own naive assumptions about the plausibility of such a project, I agreed to carry the responsibility. I was quickly humbled by the task of sorting through and editing selections for the book from the material that had been submitted by the members of the group. The task was overwhelming because of the enormous quantity of material. More significantly, however, I found that I was still too close to the experience to form an objective, coherent statement about it. Meeting with the men at Soledad had been my introduction to the horror, pain and inhumanity of the California prison system. It had been our consistent contact with these men which had sustained my energy during the strenuous two months of our scheduled meetings. Now that this contact had been severed, I was in a state of letdown combined with the angry frustration that comes to all of us when we serve witness to injustices about which we can apparently do nothing. This feeling of loss and impotence was reinforced as I re-lived the prison experience through the writings of the students and prisoners with whom I had shared such important encounters.

To the rescue came Ann Lane, a talented writer who was working at the university as a research assistant. She had had no prior experience with the penal system but she liked the idea of the book and offered her time and editorial skills for the duration of the project. We worked closely together for the remainder of the summer during which time Ann designed the book's format, selected and edited the material, and kept up my spirits with her intelligent perserverance and good humor.

The first draft of the book was near completion when Ann and I met a photographer who wanted to contribute photographs to the work. We thought it would be appropriate to include pictures of all those students and prisoners who had participated in the project and we began the arduous task of seeking permission from the Soledad Department of Corrections to allow the photographs to be taken. Through a long period of phone calls and correspondence we began to realize that we had opened a can of bureaucratic and potentially dangerous worms. We discovered that several of the prisoners had been transferred from Soledad to other penal institutions. Prison administrators were hostile to our request, summarily denying us permission and in one case indicating, threateningly it seemed, that we had no business publishing a book containing the writings of prisoners. We sought legal counsel and learned that we were safely within legal bounds in our plan for the book.

However, we began to receive word, both through the grapevine and through letters mailed to us directly from the prisoners, that several of the men from our group were receiving parole denials and being subjected to treatment which we could only construe as undue harassment. We could not know whether it was coincidence or whether it was the prison authorities' response to our plans for publication. Out of fear for the repercussions which could befall the men who had so courageously and candidly opened themselves up to us in our meetings and in their writings, the book project was shelved for nearly one year.

In the fall of 1972 I showed the manuscript to a friend, Raven Lang, who had recently published a book and in the process had formed an independent publishing company, Genesis Press. Raven was excited about the book and expressed concern that it should be published. With my interest in the project renewed, I considered again the question of the safety of those men who remained vulnerable to the arbitrary power and punishment of the prison authorities. I began to reflect heavily on the early discussions within the group at Soledad about the value of a collective publication. The consensus at that time had been 100% in favor of publication, and not one of the prisoners had opted for anonymity in the book. The men did acknowledge the dangers of speaking out to the public, but they had assured us that they wanted to go ahead with it. They had explained that as convicts their lives are continually exposed to risks of all kinds, and that as individuals each of them was continually subject to physical and psychic danger. They had insisted that to publish a book which would communicate something about their experience and ideas—a book which could encourage more and more people to get acquainted with the human life and positive energy that is contained behind our prison walls—a book which might serve as a catalyst for increasing contact between prisoners and those on the outside who could join them in a collective struggle toward a New World—that all of this was worth any risks to any of them as isolated individuals. Ultimately what each of the prisoners had communicated to us was that *everyone* must be willing to assume personal risks in a collective effort toward the collective good.

I proceeded to search out and make contact with all those prisoners who could still be located. Some of them were still at Soledad, others were confined in other penal institutions, and several had been released on parole in the fifteen months since our meetings had ended. In each case, I was reassured that their commitment to the book was still firm. Arthur Stasney, now on parole, read the manuscript in progress and gave it his endorsement. The students from the university had never ceased on their part to urge the completion of the project. Thus, after a year of withholding the collective option, I resolved to forge ahead with our book.

I was joined in the task of preparing the final draft by Scott Frankenberg, who gave me a great deal of help and support in the ensuing months. Rebecca Schiffrin and Andrew Schiffrin gave careful reading and excellent criticism to the manuscript in progress. The book's final form was influenced by suggestions and criticisms of Michael Rotkin and John Isbister. Both contributed generously as friends, mentors and manuscript consultants.

This book represents the collective experience of a group of men and women who owe their coming together to the guiding force of Dr. Ralph Guzman, who initiated the class which this book describes. He brought to us a profound understanding of the complexities of our circumstances, a rare ability to draw timid souls into meaningful dialogue with one another, a keen scholastic resourcefulness, and a deep respect for students and prisoners alike. Dr. Guzman has a serious and critical respect for the process of education. Through teaching university courses on prisons he recognized that all the theories and lectures combined could not substitute for the actual experience of entering the prison and engaging in dialogue with those who are confined therein. He recognized the learning value that such an exchange would have for both prisoners and students. Thus he successfully promoted, through many serious bureaucratic difficulties, the occasion of the class at Soledad. We who benefited most directly from his efforts will be forever grateful to him.

Finally, I join Dr. Guzman in extending gratitude to the following persons who directly or indirectly gave assistance to the organizing of the class at Soledad:

Carl Tjerandsen, Dean of the UCSC Extension; Charles Crary, Principal of the Adult Valley School, Monterey Public School System; Robert Donnelly, former Assistant Superintendent of North Facility at Soledad; Bonnie Zimmerman and Pat Patterson of UCSC Merrill College; Bruce Dancis, Souci Klein, Eddie Velasquez, James Carr,* Lorenzo Abeyta, and Jose Gonzales—all research assistants to Dr. Guzman; officers and members of the Latin American group of North Facility, who originally invited us to visit the prison.

Karlene Faith
Santa Cruz 1973

INTRODUCTION

This book is the result of an experiment in learning in which prisoners of Soledad Correctional Training Facility and students from the University of California at Santa Cruz were brought together within the prison in a class entitled Politics 190C: Utopian Studies. The class was initiated by Professor Ralph Guzman through the University of California Extension with the cooperation of the Soledad administration. As Dr. Guzman's Teaching Assistant, my task was to coordinate the organization of the class, which was co-instructed by Dr. Guzman and myself.

The university students who participated in the class at Soledad were selected by a committee which included Dr. Guzman, myself and several ex-prisoners who had entered the university as students and/or teaching and research assistants. We based our selections on past academic involvement and demonstrated interest in the United States penal system. We also wanted to provide the class with an ethnic balance; thus the UCSC component included several individuals whose racial and lower-economic backgrounds paralleled the backgrounds of the majority of the prisoners in the class. Given this preference to minority students and given the very low ethnic ratio on the university campus, the choice of UC students was accomplished with relative ease. The opposite was true in the selection of the Soledad component. From approximately 2,000 residents, only 14 could be invited to join the class. Again, the choices were made on the basis of achieving an ethnic balance—a simple criterion in light of the disproportionate number of minority prisoners at Soledad. The more difficult challenge of choosing who actually would be involved in the class was based on the individual's interest in higher education and willingness to carry a heavy academic course load. This responsibility was assumed by the coordinators of the Soledad education program. Since there is little or no record of the intellectual competence or academic motivation for most prisoners, the final selection made by the Soledad authorities was of necessity quasi random. The following section, "Autobiographies of the Contributors to this Book," identifies individually those prisoners and students who finally came together to form the class.

None of us from the university who participated in this class could have anticipated the tremendous draining of energy and spirits it would affect upon us; nor could we have known prior to the experience how dramatically rewarding it would be for us. We met once a week for two months, with each meeting lasting five hours. The UCSC group each week made the hour and one-half drive to Soledad from Santa Cruz. Travelling together, we entered the prison as a body—passing through the various security checks and metal detecting devices. Our entry into the prison was accompanied by members of the prison staff, who locked and unlocked the doors and cages through which we passed, and stood guard outside the locked room in which our class met.

The prison guards often treated us with contempt and open disdain, on several occasions "forgetting" to unlock our room until hours beyond the appointed time. The room where we met was always either stifling hot or so cold that we shared the available jackets in a futile attempt to keep warm. We were always conscious of the P.A. speakers in the room which allowed any guard or administrator to listen in on our class discussions at any time, without our consent. For the Soledad members of the class, the guards were omnipresent reminders that at any time (as happened on several occasions) they could be taken from the class setting. Treated as a herd of captive animals, the prisoners were repeatedly humiliated by the guards in our presence.

For those of us from the university, the overwhelmingly positive aspect of these meetings was our encounter and involvement with the men themselves. They represented a wide range of educational backgrounds, including one man who had a master's degree in physics. Most of the men, however, came from lower-economic backgrounds and environments. Several had grown up in Spanish-speaking communities and used English as a second language. The majority were in their twenties—the eldest being 40. They had been incarcerated for a variety of offenses and all were serving indeterminate sentences, i.e., release and parole dates determined through periodic reviews by an Adult Authority Board—a committee of prison administrators. What they had in common with one another was the stigma and experience of imprisonment and the determination to come to terms with the hideous uncertainty of their lives.

Through their encounter with the UCSC members of the class, the prisoners sought to clarify and examine the societal conditions surrounding their personal dilemmas. And by virtue of our sharing in this struggle, we too were to confront many hitherto unexamined assumptions about this world we live in. The process of our doing this together was an unfolding of inhibitions, a development of intellectual tools, the sharing of ideas and experience, and the forced acknowledgement of racial disunities and misunderstandings within our very midst. Together we searched for utopian models in an atmosphere that was the antithesis of all our private utopian fantasies.

Karlene Faith
Santa Cruz 1972

AUTOBIOGRAPHIES OF THE CONTRIBUTORS TO THIS BOOK

The Soledad/Santa Cruz Collective

ROBERTO R. ARRAS
B-24050 North Soledad

Yo soy Roberto R. Arras, *un Chicano en las Pinta de Soledad Norte. Me Torcieron por una possecion de carga y me dieron 2 a 10 anos per eso.* Since I've been here a great thing happened to me. *La Causa* has made me a *soldado por mi Raza, La Raza de Bronze. Tengo 32 anos de edad y pienso ir al colegio cuando salaza de aqui, (con suerte entre un ano). La Causa* has lit my fire and hopefully I can turn younger *chicanitos y chicanitas* on to *La Causa* for the betterment of *nuestra Linda Raza.* There are many *Chicanos,* dedicated to *La Causa,* and I hope to follow in their footsteps. Prior to my enlightenment to *La Causa* I was just a burden to my *raza; era tecato y nomás pensaba de mi y nadien mas. Soy nacido en El Paso, Texas (1939), tengo viviendo en Los desde 1948.* I was raised *en los barrios de* east Los Angeles and *en "El Jardin," en Pico Rivera, Califas.*

While doing time here I have become the Editor of *La Voz del Chicano,* a newsletter in which all the *Chicanos* here contribute articles and opinions. In a sense I was born here; I broke out of the "white shell" in which I lived. I will dedicate myself to "breaking" the white shells those *carnales y carnalas* are in *para que miran la verdad y que hagan algo por la Raza, la Familia grande.*

Yes, my fire has been lit, nothing short of death will turn it off.

My Raza, I love you and I will work for you, that is my wish, that is what I will do. *Que viva la Causa y el moviemiento. Yo Soy Chicano.*

COURTNEY LONNIE CAIN
B-26494 North Soledad

I was born in Washington, D.C., in 1950. I came to San Francisco in 1952, and I lived in the Fillmore District. I am Black. I think Black, live Black, act Black. At the present time I am studying to be a draftsman at Soledad Prison. I'm here for robbery. And I was robbing because it was the only way I could stay alive. I do have training in printing, taking pictures and mechanical drawing, but I couldn't get a job at any of these trades so I took things from people. I have graduated from high school and I'm trying to get into college at Santa Cruz. I'm a very open-minded person and I like to see things eye to eye. The outcome of my life leaves me disagreeing altogether with the U.S.A. government.

PEDRO R. CHACON
B-8747 North Soledad

I have been incarcerated for a burglary charge but I have already done more than four years because they probably feel that I am a dangerous individual as far as the elite's status quo is concerned. I come from Palm Springs in Southern California which has a distinct cross-section of economic and social circumstances, running the gamut from very poor *braceros* to multi-millionaires. There seems to be an easy comaraderie among the permanent residents but there are places which I, a brown-middle-class Catholic, can't or wouldn't dare to go and by the same token some of the super-rich Anglos couldn't safely go into certain sections of our town. Because of my dad's comfortable income bracket I can and do associate with a lot of people from Canyon Country Club and Las Palmas, which most of my friends—*Chicanos* who aren't starving but who don't have it quite as easy as I do—can't do. This gives me insight into the philosophies of the two main social classes locked in combat. I've heard and seen the stupidity with which the upper-middle-class Anglos write off *La Raza,* saying we can't amount to anything. This is my greatest hope in our battle for our rights; we will conquer.

SHERWIN L. FORTÉ
B-21899 North Soledad

I was born in Birmingham, Alabama, in 1947, in a black community where we were harassed and kept in our places by the whites. When I was 11, my mother remarried and we moved to Berkeley, California, where we lived in a black ghetto slum but I went to a semi-integrated school. It was my first experience with an integrated community and I questioned why the new school was so much better than my old one. At an early age I denounced god as being—if he existed at all—a cold and merciless person (or thing). I began a ruthless campaign denouncing those who believed in this nothing and I lost many would-be friends. I also became very racist (from about 14 to 17) but when I graduated from high school I began to understand the function of racism and it receded and gave way to communism and socialism. By the time I was 20, I was bitterly opposed to the draft and the war in Vietnam, political oppression at home and capitalism. I advocated drastic and speedy social change by any means necessary. I became part of several organizations of similar philosophy. Premature, rash and perhaps emotional and immature actions in 1969, got me convicted of assault and I was incarcerated at Soledad. This class on utopian societies has cleared up many flaws in my thinking and has provided me with invaluable insights. In short, the class has been the most beautiful experience of my prison career.

RUBEN GONZALES
B-28988 North Soledad

At the present time I am deeply involved in the *Chicano movimiento* here at Soledad. In my first few months of incarceration, truthfully speaking, I was lost like a great many of my *carnales* who first come to the *pinto*. Sure I had "homies" here, but under the circumstances which prevail in the institution, it was impossible to spend time with them as if we were still on the streets. As time went on the rest of the *carnales* here helped to educate me in terms of *Mi Raza*. Back home I was what most of those who live within the *barrio* would call a *tecato*, in which my whole purpose of being was a fix. Not really caring what went on around me or for that matter to me. Being here has opened my eyes to a great deal of the conflict which my *raza* face day-in, day-out. Problems which have kept us under the table for so long that it is almost impossible to determine just exactly when we were put there. Now many of my *carnales y carnalas* have found the crack in the wall and are willing to fight for *La Causa*. Getting back to the present, I stated before that the *carnales* here were very constructive in making a *soldado por mi Linda Raza*. Now I hold the position of Vice-Chairman of the *Chicano* group within the institution, which is dedicated toward the betterment of *La Raza*. I hope that what little I may contribute will help some *Chicano* here see things as they really are and become a *soldado y servidor de Nuestra Linda Raza*.

PHILLIP JACOBS
B-21434A North Soledad

I was born in a small rural town—Henderson, Texas, in 1947. Moving to Los Angeles in 1952, I spent the remainder of my childhood wandering around that city; my interests centered primarily around reading and enjoyment of the spices of life. My childhood was one of happiness, being the son of two wonderful black parents, who provided for my brother and my sister and me to the best of their ability; in school I was an average student with the bulk of my interest centered around history and sciences. After quitting school in 1964, I joined the U.S. Navy and embarked on the *Harry E. Hubbard,* a destroyer, for my first tour of Vietnam. Prior to this I married and the outcome of this was two wonderful sons. Although this union didn't work out the lady and I still have an understanding that our children won't be neglected. After my discharge from the Navy, I had many plans and ideas I wished to pursue, but I ran afoul of the law while attending the junior college in Los Angeles where I was majoring in political science. My clean record and employment weren't enough to prevent my coming to prison. I'm a person, though incarcerated. My dream of the future is to prevent my younger black brothers the pitfalls in which I became entrapped. The most intense desire I have is to acquire the means of bringing about changes in the injustices of our society. This class has been rewarding to me in many ways. The help provided me by the class, especially by Karlene, has been most rewarding.

5

MICHAEL LEE
B-24542-A North Soledad

I am an Asian-American born 24 years ago in Los Angeles. My education has been based mostly on my own initiative. My background consisted more or less of low-riding, narcotics, etc. I have seen through experience that my background is irrelevant to my present state of mind and position; the new culture prevails, for it is Mao's destiny. The peace-loving people shall attain their liberation and freedom. My life is dedicated to bringing about the ultimate goal of all-freedom for all people by any means necessary. I wish to express revolutionary solidarity with all of you who are either actively struggling or supporting the People's struggle for total World-Wide Liberation and Peace.

WILLIAM EARL LUTE
B-24871-B North Soledad

I'm a drug addict. I've spent over four of my last five years inside a penal institution. My crimes have been passing checks to support my habit and/or possessing narcotics. I'm labelled a criminal. I'm 22 and I've been labelled a criminal for five years. I'm beginning to live up to my social image. As my life wastes away here, I devote all my energies to retaining my sanity. No, I'm not on the brink of "mental illness"—not anymore than my fellow convicts. It's a daily battle here to retain my self-respect and sanity as an individual. With the other thousand men imprisoned here, I am exposed to biased, bigoted and sick personalities who have complete authority over my every "privilege." I'm from a lower-middle-class white family in Modesto, California. I've been a rebel or problem child since I was eleven. I blame myself and the whole society for my anti-social behavior. We must change our system soon, before it is too late. Not for me—I'm probably too late—but my children— I'll be released someday and I'll make another whole-hearted attempt to live within your rules. My chances are one in a hundred and I know it. But perhaps I'll be that one. It's my only hope.

THEODORE MARTINEZ
B-24565 North Soledad

I have lived in San Jose, California, for 27 years and although I have lived under the white man's law I have never tried to understand my own experience. My family is very close-knit so I have never tried to relate to the system and have lived most of my years as a criminal against the society in which I live. Lately I have opened my mind to knowledge and the reason for its use. I feel, and my family feels, that education is the way for betterment of one's goals. But being a *Chicano* I have been misled and have rebelled against the laws, ending up in the state prison. I now want to re-build my life to the structure of someone I so desire to be. My older brother Joe has completed six years of college and has really become someone. My younger brother and sister still don't understand this world and I hope to make them aware. I shall do my utmost to make all my *Raza* understand themselves in order to achieve a good political and educational program so that we can fight the system at its own game. My educational background is very broad because I have gone through a lot of schools. But while being incarcerated I have almost completed high school and I have been involved in two college courses. I am going to enter San Jose State when I am released.

STANLEY EDWARD MAYABB
B-24715 North Soledad

I was born in Hollywood, California, in 1950. I was raised in a white, lower-middle-class family and environment. My parents fortunately never divorced. I have three brothers, aged 14, 12 and 7, and a sister 3 years old. I graduated from the Boys' Republic High School in Chino, California, in 1967. I did one year of college work at Cerritos Junior College (general education and police science). Since coming to prison in 1968, I have become a member of the American Humanist Association and the World Citizens League. I am very disillusioned with the current establishment and I'm now a staunch socialist.

RUBEN REYNA
B-21734 North Soledad

Quisiera en primer lugar dar a la libertad del uso de mi nombre. Para el uso en que sea necesitado.

Yo Ruben R. Reyna, de Alamo, Tejas, me encountro en el presente, Pinto en Las Prisiones de California—Soledad.

Entre mis anos en el campo vagando he expiriensado muchisimas aventuras. Soy pobre y por esa razon es que me sali de mi casa para lasciudedes donde se encurentra el juego del criminal. Y es por eso que yo y muchos de mis carnales Chicanos nos encontramos en estos lugares.

Pero yo como el resto de muchos otros carnales. He llegado a un punto en mi vida en que miro que es necesitado ayudar a mi gente. Y quisiera tener suficiente sabiduria para nuestro mejoramiento. Tengo experiencias para poner al dispuesto de quien las necesite. Pero necesitamos a ustedes aqui para formar un puente para nuestros dos mundos y el beneficio del mundo tercero—Ya no somos convictos pero Prisooneros Politicos—para el mejoramiento de la gente.

Aunque ya no estaremos physicamente juntos, nuestros corazones estan siempre con ustedes.

7

[I, Ruben R. Reyna of Alamo, Texas, am presently in Soledad Prison. During my years travelling from one place to another in the fields, I experienced many adventures. I am poor, which is why I left my home for the city, where the "criminal's game" is found. And why many of my *Chicano* blood brothers and I are in these places.

But like other brothers, I've come to a time in my life in which I see the need for helping my people. I'd like to have enough wisdom for our improvement. I have experiences to put at the disposal of those who need them. But we need you people here to build a bridge between our two worlds and for the benefit of the Third World. We are no longer convicts but political prisoners for the advancement of the people.

Although we will no longer be with you physically, our hearts are always with you.—Ed. trans.]

RICHARD RISHER
B-21915 North Soledad

Who am I, and why . . . Wow. Born in Houston, Texas, 29 years ago, my family migrated to the Watts section of Los Angeles when I was about five years old. So as a starting point, you might say I have Texas roots, and Watts soul. Being the third of four sons, my father was the first to fall victim to the inequities of the system and the negative overwhelming pressures of the ghetto (i.e., being denied employment and opportunities and his dignity as a man, he split, abandoned the family when I was about seven. And was sucked into the illusionary, insulating world of alcoholics. Perhaps I should say forced into that world, for I don't really think he had any choice—taking into account the limited psychological and political resources he had at his disposal), and we were raised by a dynamic black woman named Velma Lee Risher. We called her Mother. Watts in the fifties was the epitome of an asphalt jungle, and my childhood was both rough and rewarding. I say rewarding, because many of the experiences of my youth are the basis on which I have developed a rather substantial political and social consciousness at this stage of my life, a tattered and misguided life to be sure. The gang culture provided me my first political experiences. Internal power struggles; territorial disputes; war councils—and leadership. I've always been a very intense person, having an extremely large capacity for self-indulgence. Also, I was small and skinny, which needless to say, produced a "runt complex." As such, I always thought I had to do things better or more bizarre than my comrades.

Having two "big" brothers reinforced my image, and at a very early age I was off and running, and had a head-on collision with the local constabulary at the age of nine—15 counts of GTA (grand theft auto) . . . I couldn't drive and didn't particularly have an interest in cars. But I always had a few smarts which led to my being accepted by comrades four and five years my senior.

I could hot-wire the cars and they could drive; a very working relationship. From that time to the present, I have been on either probation or parole . . .

It was in prison that I began to understand that I had some intelligence. It was then, at eighteen years old that my life began to change—in the direction of political and social understanding. At Soledad in 1960 I was exposed to comrades who knew and could see what the game was all about. However, my infant consciousness was not enough to save me from the onslaught of unchanged negative conditions back in the community . . . and I was hooked on heroin and running like a dog in 17 months.

I met a dynamic psychiatrist in 1967, who happened to be a brother. He told me some things about the value of me, the intrinsic value of Richard C. Risher. And after a couple of confinements to Los Angeles Psychiatric Hospital—and subsequent relapse to drugs—I headed north for commitment to Napa State Hospital. Before I could commit myself I was arrested for the armed robbery for which I'm now serving time: 5 to life.

While lying in a cell in the Sacramento County Jail, amidst my own vomit, blood and bile; I made a commitment to myself, my family, and my people. It was at that moment that I spoke to the powers that be, to the gods, that if I made it through this ordeal alive—I would make a significant contribution. I was by no means jiving . . . that was the turning point in my life—I was physically in prison the next day.

Like magic things begin to happen to and for me. I hadn't completely regained my strength from "kicking" but on taking the many tests one gets on entering prison, I was astonished to learn that I had an IQ of 135 . . . Can you imagine that? My last years in school, my grades had deteriorated to D's and F's and I was kicked out, only to discover that I really did have sense.

I began to read everything . . . Everything I tried paid off with dividends . . . I organized and chaired floundering groups . . . initiated programs . . . The more I attempted the more I could accomplish . . .

As I see it now, my plans are to obtain a degree in political science, which I think will give, in addition to my experiences, an even greater understanding of the socio-political situation, and thus increase my effectiveness in such areas as penal reform, social reform, etc. Always know that for peace and power, we must commit ourselves to struggle and unity of purpose.

ARTHUR STASNEY
B-31450 North Soledad

I was born in 1932 in Seattle—archetypal middle-class upbringing. In 1954, I graduated from the California Institute of Technology with a Master of Science degree in physics. Handsomely paid for 13 years by various departments of defense contractors for planning megadeath murder of women and children; dropped out in 1968. Handsomely rewarded with free room, board and clothing by the State of California in 1970, for peddling acid. It beats killing civilians but the risks are greater. Well, as Lenny Bruce said, America is a place that accords more honor to a general than a whore.

MONA BURNS
College V, UCSC

I was born 35 years ago and raised in rural Iowa. It was a poorer and a richer life than most of the cliches suggest. My parents were poor when I was born, and only just achieving stability when I graduated from high school. In addition we were not among the community's insiders, the people whose families had lived and owned land there for generations. They had the land and they were all more or less related as well. They tended to see the rest of us as transients; there would always be farm hands and school teachers and truck drivers, but the names and faces change. There were no blacks or browns, no Catholics or Jews, and virtually no strangers in all my early experience. There were few occasions of excitement or high drama.

But the quiet facts of life were all around us, and in such a community one participates in them. Everyone's birth and death, illness, marriage, accomplishments and debts were community business. We made no frantic search for "relationships." If communications with one another were somewhat stylized, they were also predictable and usually gentle.

I married a college student who subsequently became a minister and then an Army chaplain. We have moved a number of times and met a great variety of people. We have three children. I don't miss the old home town (they were right about us being transients) but sometimes I long for that sense of community. There is strength for feeble humans in shared tasks and shared disasters. If I have a "goal" in the traditional sense, it is to help make this sense of sharing available to the modern, mobile people in a setting of chaos.

EUGENE CALHOUN
Cowell College, UCSC

I was born in 1950, in Oakland, California, where I spent most of my life. I consider myself quite lucky because I was able to avoid a lot of the bullshit that a black person has to go through while growing up. My parents sent me through 12 years of Catholic school and I didn't have to deal with the madness of the Oakland public school system. (And I've outgrown the indoctrination I received in the Catholic school.) I was luckier than some of my partners; I was able to get away before the cops came. I've always been interested in people—wondered what was going on in their heads. At age 7, I began asking, Why is it that people can't get along? Why can't they just be cool? I'm still asking that question. And just now beginning to find the answers.

10

And just beginning to do something about it. In high school I became interested in theatre as a political tool, a way of educating the people. I hope to be able to use it to its fullest. I'm majoring in Afro-American literature and theatre at UCSC. I hope to form a community theatre in Oakland after I graduate. I have also, since being involved with the Soledad Defense Committee, become interested in going to law school.

JOAQUIN CASTRO
Cowell College, UCSC

I was born 22 years ago in Dinuba, California, a rural town in the San Joaquin Valley. I came from a Chicano family very similar to most of the families in the area. The main function of these families is to provide the labor to harvest the abundant fruit in this valley. After attending the public schools provided for the children of this type of family, after years of digesting cultural insults such as having my name changed from Joaquin to Jack by an enlightened teacher who couldn't pronounce Joaquin. I somehow managed to secure EOP funds provided by the "benevolent" state to attend the University. I am now majoring in Politics and trying desperately to stay in this first year. If I survive, my purpose will be to do as much as possible to overthrow the American capitalistic system.

ALMA COTA
Crown College, UCSC

I am one of four children born to Ricardo and Francisca Cota. I am from a migrant background and come from Calexico, California. We were ten persons migrating around the state—a grandmother and a cousin moved with us also. By luck I got accepted to the University of California and am now a senior majoring in sociology.

BEN DUNN
Merrill College, UCSC

I was born in 1941, to a working class family in New York. The schools I attended gave me a woefully inadequate education. I maintain that it was not an education I received but rather a training—a training to make me a part of and a perpetrator of this social system. I came to Santa Cruz in 1963, seeking work and a new life. I found both, but still very much within the system. The military soon claimed me—the U.S. Navy. After serving two years of active duty, including four months in Vietnam, I returned home. Now home was

Santa Cruz, and my old job at Pacific Gas and Electric. The military experience left many latent doubts in my mind about this social order. The inhumanity of that whole way of life disgusted me; however, I could see that with slight modifications straight American working class society wasn't much different. In 1968, a fulltime student career began for me at Cabrillo Junior College in Aptos, California. I transferred to UCSC in 1970, majoring in Asian History. I also feel committed to study American society, to promote revolutionary ideals through radical social change. I feel most of us have been in a prison of the mind, just living in America. I want very much to tear down the mental and physical prisons in this society.

ROBBIE FREEMAN
Merrill College, UCSC

I come from a poor family of Blacks, all of whom have emigrated from the south in my lifetime. I use the word "family" quite generally because it must include eight aunts and uncles, all of whom have cared for my sister and myself in the absence of my mother (deceased) and my father (estranged).

I was educated in the ghetto and school always seemed so simple. For eleven years I was not expected to think but to regurgitate information because that's as well as the teachers thought we could perform. I guess I regurgitated well; I was an honor student. In the eleventh grade I met a Black teacher from Beverly Hills High School, and one day he took me to school with him. I met some freshmen and sophomores whose intelligence baffled me, and I decided I couldn't be denied my first opportunity to learn. So I graduated from Beverly High, and with those amazingly misrepresentative grades from the white teachers in the ghetto (who were astonished that I regurgitated so well) I was in the top five percent of a class of 550. Thank you, white teachers in the ghetto.

From there I went to college while most of my contemporaries were getting busted or married. The marriages are understandable, but the arrests? Were my brothers being tracked to prison? I think they are, and since I can't tackle the conflict between a subculture (the ghetto) ethos and society's traditions (a conflict which causes the imprisonment of so many Blacks), I'm centering my studies on their most influential meeting place: the law.

REBECA ALICIA LOPEZ
Merrill College, UCSC

I was born 22 years ago in San Francisco, Califas, Aztlan. I lived an exciting, dangerous life until my family made the big move south to the suburb of Redwood City, where I at least had a better chance of growing up, though it was a warped, unrealistic atmosphere. Fortunately a recent influx of

Chicanos and other people of color plus the growth of Venceremos College and its various community organizations have made Redwood City a more relevant place to grow and learn in. An uneventful stint in high school led me to the College of San Mateo where I was part of a token Third World program in a scared, rich white junior college above the mansions of Hillsborough, California. The inevitable liquidation of the program, and its students, brought me to a new reality and conviction that since my presence was not desired in college then I would do everything possible to stay in college and get out with whatever it is white students get out with. Admittedly without much effort on my part I happened into the University of California at Disneyland (Santa Cruz) where I am now completing my junior year majoring in Social Anthropology. I hope to finish up here and try to get into some graduate school, probably because so many people have told me I can't do it. Also, I can see that a few more pieces of paper will allow me the mobility and possibly the bread I'll need to do what I want for my *Raza* on the street and in the joint.

FRANCISCO MANTUA
Merrill College, UCSC

I am an Asian-American who did not grow up with the material luxuries of the American middle class. Fortunately, my father had attended a western university and he and my mother instilled in their children the value of education for attaining upward economic and social mobilization. Unfortunately, it was I who failed to distinguish between acculturation, an eclectic process, and assimilation, an imitative process.

It was not until my separation from the service and subsequent return to academia that I have been able to analyze and articulate my past, present, and future. Some parts of my past I have just now begun to appreciate and accept, without having to make excuses out of a sense of shame nor formulate elaborate rationales for a personality which is not my own. The catalyst for much of my present consciousness was my tour of service in the U.S. Army. I was a draft dodger for seven months—not because of protest over the Vietnam war, nor even the military institution, as I was totally inarticulate in such matters—but I felt that the Army (military) was repulsive to me as an individual. Mine was a selfish, narrow viewpoint at best. However, partly because I lacked any sort of political and social articulation, I soon became a very enthusiastic—in every way—member of the military. In short order, within 11 months of my induction I progressed from draftee to advanced Infantry Training Honor Graduate to commissioned officer in the Armoured Branch. This led me to volunteer for Airborne Training (definite elitist feeling) and for a command in combat. I served in Vietnam as a platooon leader, executive officer and acting company commander in an infantry division and a separate airborne brigade.

I believe that my reaction to the service is not unlike many ethnics who found the military experience a love-hate relationship. It ranged from a pride of belonging, a problem endemic to those coming from ruptured cultures; the intense feeling of camaraderie among fighting men, black, white, brown, red, yellow; to the deep bitter anguish of seeing (from this brown man's eyes) that the standard of living of the Vietnamese whom we were liberating was not all that much lower than that of the poor in America; the ranks of *combat* units filled predominantly by *color* (where was the white majority?).

We who were of color (especially Asian-Americans) were told by our peers, "You're different, man." We certainly are different; we do not live in the same neighborhoods, we do not have the same job opportunities, and we do not have the same educational opportunities, if any at all.

As an individual I can no longer feel bitter toward myself for having been so effectively socialized into accepting the values of the dominant culture which does not take racial disparities into account. But I do now share in the collective bitterness toward a system that grants privileges to some while denying those same privileges to others.

GARY PERNELL
College V, UCSC

I was born 19 years ago in Long Beach, California, where my parents and and sister were the major influences on my life. My younger years, although well-provided for, were filled with the usual competition and blind confusion. I now hold the schools and educational system responsible for not acknowledging the political realities. My own crude recognition that I could not receive an education that I considered *relevant* from an education factory— that was only succeeding in keeping me away from people I wanted to know and subjects I wanted to learn—prompted my decision to go to continuation school for my junior year in high school. This experience opened me to many possibilities for my life; since I only went half-days I had a lot of time to be involved in musical, political and cultural activities. At 17, I left home and attended Cabrillo Junior College, in Aptos, California. During this period, I was thoroughly exposed to a radical analysis of society. I have always felt there should be equality between people. I now see that this cannot occur by merely wanting it. Equality now means economic, political, and social collectivity. It is toward these goals that my education is now focused.

PLEZENA YVONNE SHACK
Merrill College, UCSC

I was born December 15, 1948, in Pittsburg, California, to Pleasant and Virginia Lee Shack. I lived in Rodeo, California, for 12 years then moved to Berkeley where I now reside. I am currently attending the University of California at Santa Cruz where I major in political science. I am a senior at Merrill College and will graduate in June of 1972. I plan to go into law because I feel the practice of law will be the best way to serve my Black brothers and sisters. I've wanted to be an attorney since the age of 8 or 9. I first became aware of my Black self while attending Merritt Junior College in Oakland, California. While attending Merritt, Huey was arrested and at that time I first came to understand the injustices that Blacks suffer and the way Blacks survive from day to day. From that time until eternity I fight for our right to be free. All power to the people. Love and revolution.

DEIRDRE STONE
Cowell College, UCSC

I was born in Oakland, California, twenty-two years ago. I'm from the privileged class. I've always had what I needed and never known hunger. I find this type of life merely existence, and made the vow sometime ago not to close my eyes to the oppression around me. More recently I came to the realization that I too was oppressed by the hand which so willingly fed me. I felt my oppression as a woman and as a child of the sterile bourgeoisie. So I began to act. Now it is my revolutionary duty and my creative joy. No way to turn around. Through my work with the Soledad Brothers Defense Committee I've been introduced to the horrors of institutionalized facism and repression—the prisons. I feel that the brothers and sisters held captive behind the walls and steel of "correctional" institutions are the true revolutionary vanguard and I will follow their counsel. Only those who have been to hell, suffered as no other group of beings have been made to suffer, know the madness for what it really is. They must lead our struggle. All Power to the People. Straight ahead in Love and Revolution.

DEBRA ANN WALTON
Merrill College, UCSC

I was born in 1952, in Santa Cruz, California. I attended elementary, junior high, high school and the first year of college in Santa Cruz. Lived a few summers in L.A. with relatives. Home in Santa Cruz is in a lower middle-class neighborhood with a reasonable number of Blacks. I disliked school from the beginning. Later I began to realize the true value of education, but I still couldn't get into school and I'm glad I didn't get too far into that shit. The University is better but I really have to leave Santa Cruz soon. My level of consciousness has just recently turned toward my being Black and relating to my people in a useful way. This past year I have been trying to reach a revolutionary level of consciousness but it is hard in Santa Cruz because of the unreal summer-camp atmosphere.

RANKO YAMADA
Merrill College, UCSC

Born and raised in Stockton, California. Eighteen years old, a Sansei, an Amerasian. Our family household was gathered around a culturally Buddhist tradition. Each morning I woke to burning incense and light bell tones of a minature gong. The first portion of each meal was, and is, given before a family shrine—a ritual of respect to our ancestors. My attitude is probably more Buddhistic than I realize. I was the stereotype, quiet Japanese, a "good student," etc. Many of my roots are embedded in Chinatown, San Francisco: luaus; dances; a neighborhood of death; TB; reds, and undercover cops. And trips. Lots and lots of trips. From ratted hair and straight black skirt, cruising and visiting friends in juvenile hall (about age 12 to 15) to a white social trip, to white hippie trip. And lastly, and permanently, no longer a "trip"—being part of the Asian movement. One mind and body in constant struggle to raze the structure that exists on the blood and suffering of our people—a structure that does not allow us to know who we really are.

RALPH GUZMAN
Professor, UCSC

Dr. Guzman was born in Moroleon, Guanajuato, Mexico, in 1924. Immigrating to the United States in 1929, Dr. Guzman's family worked in the agricultural fields of the American southwest. During World War II, he served in the U.S. Merchant Marines and in the U.S. Navy. Dr. Guzman attended East Los Angeles Junior College, UCLA, and the California State College at Los Angeles. He received a doctorate in political science at UCLA. In 1962-63 Dr. Guzman served in the U.S. Peace Corps as Associate Director in the Republic of Venezuela and later in Peru. Since 1969 Dr. Guzman has been an Associate Professor in Politics and Community Studies at the University of California at Santa Cruz. He is presently serving a Chancellor's appointment to develop a college devoted to ethnic studies. Dr. Guzman has held advisory positions on federal, state and local levels of government. He is a regular speaker at universities, professional conferences, and community organizations around the United States. And he has been active in organizations dedicated to the advancement of the Mexican-American community. Dr. Guzman has contributed articles to numerous scholarly journals and government reports and he has been the author of several major publications, notably, *The Mexican-American: Our Second Minority*. (New York: Macmillan, The Free Press).

KARLENE FAITH
Graduate Student, UCSC

The eldest of six children, I was born 33 years ago in Saskatchewan, Canada. We moved to the States in the late forties, when my father became the pastor of a church in Montana. I lived my adolescence in a downtown house, a stone's throw from seven bars, a pool hall, a religious revival group, the county jail, and the town library. In that neighborhood I learned to love soul and gospel music, rebels, and books; and I learned to despise alcohol and to fear men in uniforms. Wild and wanting to be free, I struck out on my own while still in high school. By age 18 I had agonized or rejoiced my way through jobs as a cook and waitress, secretary, pianist, and radio programmer; Bohemian life in a communal attic; youth organizing projects; hepatitis; and a year of college as a music major. I was married in 1957 to a college friend who became a teacher and coach; we were together through 15 years of good times and hard times before finally separating this year.

Over the years we became the parents of three sons and one daughter—four beautiful, fine people who I cherish more than I can say. My "other family"—parents, sisters, brothers—scattered across the globe through the years, like poor but determined gypsies. We seem to grow closer and closer with the passing of time and I turn to them constantly for clarity and inspiration and friendship. During the sixties my husband worked with American schools overseas, and with our children we lived and worked and studied for five exciting years in Europe and East Africa. We "got culture," crossed cultures, and came face to face with devastating poverty and exploitation wrought by imperialist foreign policy. In 1966 I read Simone de Beauvoir, packed our bags, said goodbye to Ethiopia, and came with the kids to Santa Cruz, where I reentered college as a freshwoman. I majored in anthropology, and we spent one summer in the West Indies doing field study with the Ras Tafarians, a political/religious group in Jamaica which has never stopped struggling against the colonialist/imperialist repressions on their island. For the past several years I've been doing practice with prisoner support groups and developing theory with marxist study collectives. Another major energy commitment grew from my kids' difficult experiences with public schools, confirming my own memory of schools as poor substitutes for education; we've worked hard, together with other people in the community, to form good education alternatives. Through the women's movement I've come to better understand, at the deepest gut level, the dialectic of the personal and the political. With sisters I find joy and courage in collective struggle against sexism and in facing our own internalized contradictions. I find it easier these days to militate against racism, chauvinism, ageism, imperialism, and authoritarianism as very real, life-negating manifestations of a capitalist system which we must combat as creatively and carefully as we can, at the most profound levels of our existence. I feel good with myself and with my comrades as I participate in that process of building a new, a better world. We live with a system that mindlessly hurts people. We need to learn how to be good to each other. It seems that simple and that complicated to me. Meanwhile, I treasure every minute we find to celebrate with music and food and love and affirmation, as we continue together in that liberating process.

ROBBIE'S POEM

Robbie Freeman
Merrill College, UCSC

Four Cement walls and
Three locked doors; they,
In a second,
For a moment
Accosted me with their restraint.
And it was a frightful second
And an anxious moment
Until I,
Glancing around the large room
At others from UCSC,
Realized that, of course,
"They couldn't keep me here."

Which drew my attention to
The men
Because, unfortunately,
They could keep them there.
And I was immediately confronted
With something that, before now
I could only sympathize with and
My sympathy was a "feeling"
About something I'd never felt;
Something each man must feel
The moment his cell door clicks:
The indignation of . . .
The fear of . . .
The pain of and/or . . .
The resignation to
His inescapable entombment.

Thirteen nice guys
Thirteen calm men
Calm,
Except for the natural nervousness
That we all felt in this
uncommon encounter.
For a while,
I couldn't relate it—
These "nice guys"
To what I know about "O" wing;
These composed conservative men
To the arrogant revolutionaries of "O" wing—.

We talked individually to each other
And we all talked "Utopia" for a while
Then I saw
The obvious answer:
I'd sat next to a man
Who was slightly saddened
By our coming
He was being transferred to
Chino
The next day—not to Quentin—
To Chino (and he wouldn't be able to take the class).

The exact words of the conversation
Are foggy to me now
But the tone of it,
The man's deepest sentiments,
Were crouched
Under
compromise.
A compromise of thoughts
(His reactionary politics) plus
A compromise of action
(He "played it cool" and "did what they said")
Equals a transfer to Chino
(He's on the way out)

Consequent ambivalent emotions flared inside me
I was happy for the brother
He'd played the game right
And soon he would "win"
(As much as one can win
In this kind of match)
And I was also angry
That he hadn't stood up
That he hadn't tried to
Change the Institution
(As *little* effect as it would've had)
That he wasn't revolutionary
(He's not a George Jackson)
That he *had* compromised
(And had not contested)
Then,
I realized that I was angry because
He had not
Sacrificed himself
Or his chances at
"Another crack at life"

And in the end,
I shook the Brother's hand
and smiled
and said goodbye.

THE JOURNAL
(April 5 to June 2, 1971)

This section relates the unfolding experience of the class as it was expressed by all of us who were there. Arthur Stasney and I had kept journals of the class for our individual use. These journals are reprinted here on opposing sides of the page, with relevant excerpts from the class discussions printed in between. These excerpts, as well as the essays printed in the following section, were selected from a vast quantity of writing which was submitted by members of the class. All the members of the class had kept records of our meetings. Each individual had also submitted written responses to the required class readings (Aldous Huxley, *Island*; B. F. Skinner, *Walden Two;* Erich Fromm, *The Sane Society;* Hedgepeth and Stock, *The Alternative*) and to related topics which the readings generated. We looked for those individual statements which best reflected the recurring themes of the class as they were collectively raised.

We have used this "literary-collage" format because the material describes a simultaneous experience from a variety of perspectives. We felt that to offer the material in a conventional sequential form would lose the spirit of the class. As it stands, each page of The Journal holds certain integrity for all of us who were present. For example, it exposes the contradictions and disagreements within the context in which they occurred; it reveals the social and intellectual fragmentation which we experienced with one another as well as the moments and hours of continuity and solidarity.

Readers may choose to read one column through from page to page, start to finish, and then return to read the second, third and fourth columns in conventional page order. Our hope, however, is that the reader will establish a rhythm for reading across the page and digesting simultaneously the diverse material just as it occurred within the prison meetings.

EXCERPTS FROM STUDENT ESSAYS

I cannot conceive of prisons in a utopian society.

Sherwin Forté
B-21899 Soledad

KARLENE'S JOURNAL
Monday, April 5, 1971

Ralph and I meet with Bob Donnelly—Deputy Superintendent of North Facility (shorter terms, younger guys than Central inmates). Over a rare hamburger lunch in a staff cafeteria, we present him with Ralph's ideas for the course. Hospitable and genteel—he refers us to Non-Prison, revealing his interest in prison-reform literature. Tells us that from the Politics 190c reading list, only Jackson and Cleaver should not be brought to the inmates, although they can purchase them on their own from the prison bookstore. We're joined by Chuck Crary, a public educator who is contracted to develop prison education programs. He's cordial, warm, gracious. My knife slips and he enjoys our little joke about college radicals "coming prepared." He seems to have a keen sense of the prisoners' needs—sensitive to the dilemmas. All of us move to the conference room passing through electric doors with guards recording our entries. Joined by several other Soledad staff members, we discuss the class—when we'll meet, who will participate. Ralph has emphasized the rigorous reading/writing/thinking demands that will fall on the students. Shall any of them come from Central? One of the men (who works on in-prison education programs) says, "No—there aren't any there who are bright enough." Crary is concerned with egalitarian selection—avoid giving a few men all the benefits. The other man says, "What the hell—give it to whoever can hack it. So what? this isn't apple pie—only the top dogs can make it." Another man worries about losing his room (used for prisoner orientation) to the class. Ralph suggests an additional weekly meeting time for inmates to independently discuss class experiences and materials. Crary and Donnelly worry about the inmates' ability to handle a meeting by themselves for a very long time. Compromise: we'll provide an orientation for their individual

We are so very far from a utopian society, that it is tantamount to fantasy to attempt a description of this type of society. Nevertheless one must attempt to formulate the essential requirements of this society if he has any concern whatever for the highly disturbing trend of oppression which is utilized by the "petit bourgeoisie" to keep the masses in their place. Any person who feels that he has to do something big to help the cause, upon examination of the obstacles confronting him, is almost overwhelmed by the apparent futility of that task.

Pedro Chacon
B-8747 Soledad

ARTHUR'S JOURNAL
Monday, April 12, 1971 (First Meeting)

The subject was human needs—a concensus was taken: ten primary needs and fourteen associated key words—I won't dignify them with the term "secondary needs"—were taken from the concensus:

PRIMARY NEEDS (In order, maybe?)	ASSOCIATED KEY WORDS
Love	Privacy
Communication	Mutual respect
Individuality	Compassion
Companionship	Ability to love
Education	Equality
Sex	Diversity
Aesthetics	Sense of future
Laws	Leisure
Religion	Creativity
Recreation	Expression
	Release of tension
	Being appreciated
	Desire
	Free choice

I hope not too much time is devoted to "Utopian Prisons"—objects approximately as real as two-sided triangles . . . will we get hung up in questions related to the transformation of the ghetto—the *barrio*—the inner city— whatever—into suburbia, with breezeway, two station wagons and microwave oven—thereby achieving a sort of relative utopia? Or will we assail the question of the more formidable and fundamental agonies that afflict society, affluent and deprived alike? Was the thought lurking anywhere that this class might represent a microcosm of society—ethnically balanced—in which tiny mirror some of the problems of society at large might be reflected?

Arthur Stasney
B-31450 Soledad

Karlene's Journal (cont'd.)

meetings during our regular class meeting, after which Donnelly will schedule times for them to meet alone. (He never does.) They all respect Ralph—call him "Dr. Guzman," a title which, he says, gets used more in one day at Soledad than in a month at the University. They listen to him, respectful of his academic expertise and personal commitment. But—he believes there's a reciprocal game: they worry about his potential effect, i.e., nurturing dissatisfaction among the inmates—and he must exercise unusual constraint. Donnelly agrees to allow several inmates a pass so that they can visit the campus class—cites an episode at Monterey Penninsula College—a girl so unwilling to believe the inmates' account of their prison experience—can't believe things aren't worse than the inmates say they are. Crary says he would be delighted to come and serve on a panel. [Crary does come and offered in Ralph's Politics 190c class on campus an exceptionally well-articulated statement on his experience with the California penal system. For the duration of the quarter I continued to make query to Donnelly—by letter, by phone, and once-a-week, in-person conversation at Soledad—about the promise to let the inmates come to the campus. Plans are repeatedly made and broken. They never make it.]

Monday, April 12, 1971 (First Meeting)

We file into a small cage which locks behind us—the bars before us are opened by a guard and we enter the "visiting room." An ethnically mixed group—14 inmates, 13 students, Ralph and myself are seated in a prearranged circle of chairs.

Arthur's Journal (cont'd.)

Somebody commented on the failure of modern religion (I think) stating that its failing lay in its being ritual without substance. All it takes to bring this argument to a screeching halt is to think about religion that was all substance—however ephemeral—and no ritual. Ritual is as much a need—and perhaps much more—than substance; that is why religion has developed as it has. The decline in the influence of religion has paralleled its decline in ritual content; the Catholics have made out a little better than the domestic competition because I allege, they have a lot more mumbo-jumbo. Anyone for Houston and Masters?

Well, they got to the nitty-gritty fast. Karlene was exhuberantly flashing on it; she phrased it something like "the goal is the quest itself."—Which I take to mean that it isn't the terminus of the road that matters (we all know what that is anyway), it is what happens on the way. As MLS put it, "There aren't any answers; there are only the questions and how you feel about them." The shortest and longest dissertation on record on this topic are respectively Dylan: "He who is not busy being born is busy dying" and Hesse: (Here follows all of *Magister Ludi*).

What are some other references on utopian societies (other than the course texts and other than Thoreau?)—I am particularly interested in modern—maybe even ultra-modern (post 1960) works. "The Utopiates?" Look it up. See a million articles in the underground press.

What exactly does the discussion of human needs have to do with the idea of a utopian society? I hope it is obvious: a utopian society is one which is based on the fulfilling of these needs (and is significantly successful, or it will be deemed a failed attempt at a utopian society—the word implies a reasonable degree of success.)

If a flower that you planted in your toilet doesn't grow due to lack of sunlight and nutrients, do you change the flower to grow on a severely reduced diet or do you change the environment to be more conducive to the plant's health and life?

Sherwin L. Forté
B-21899 Soledad

What we have today (and I have already admitted my inability to divorce myself from the reality of *now*) is a society which guarantees (utopia?) its people enough to eat and a longer life and then exposes them to lethal radioactivity, pollution, war . . . such a society is not moving upward toward utopia: rather it is moving sideways toward a cliff. . .

Richard Risher
B-21915 Soledad

Albeit various individual churches have been able to break away from dependency on the "system" and from its co-option of the people: on a massive scale, religion has developed into a tool perpetuating racism, sexist attitudes and oppression.

Ranko Yamada
Merrill UCSC

Freedom—I imagine its essence in terms of a lifting up. A human being rising out of something (be it ignorance, greed, cruelty, shackles, hunger, pain) and placing his/her soul on firm ground. I believe that a person is capable of knowing he is free. It is possible for an individual to possess his freedom (psychic) and remain chained to the existing conditions surrounding him. This type of freedom is valid, it is a good thing, for the person who is virtually possessed (i.e., the brothers and sisters within the penitentiary) but it is not adequate for the *collective* of human beings, on an external level.

People *have the right* to exist unburdened by physical necessities—the lack of which renders him helplessly chained to and dependent on the generosity and whims of another. Freedom extends its hand to duty. A certain amount of other-directedness insures the continuation of freedom—liberty is freedom bounded by the walls of the collective good...

Deirdre Stone
Cowell UCSC

Karlene's Journal (cont'd.)

They're jumping way ahead—getting right into it—everyone seems ready to talk. In the afternoon, Donnelly comes in and gives us a lecture about the rules and regulations of a prison: don't bring dope; don't deliver letters

Arthur's Journal (cont'd.)

I suggest that a utopian society by definition is one structured to minimize some sort of weighted average (over all its members) of the coercion (per unit time) to which each member is subjected. Behold how nicely this definition encompasses the points developed by the young lady [Robbie] who observed the evident fact that any society must involve considerable restraint on absolute individual freedom ("every time you make a friend, you take on obligations . . . ") and I will add that you restrict your available choice of behavior patterns.

Can we use this droll definition to shed any illumination on the agonizing, often-raised, border-line case: laws against physically-addicting drugs (if one prefers, smack, period)? I don't think we can provide a definite answer, but we can focus on the essence of the issue, which is often overlooked. The debates often center on whether smack is physically harmful (I am not talking about withdrawal; I'm talking about smack in plentiful supply). In accord with our principle, it doesn't matter in the least whether or not smack is harmful. The issue is: Is it voluntary? This is rather a matter of definition. I am presuming (here I speak, mercifully, from hearsay) that a profound case may be made for the theory that its physiological effects make smack at least in the advanced stages of usage decidedly an agent of coercion. We may wish to exclude self-initiated, chemical coercion without external human agency from our definition, thereby precipitating anti-smack laws into the sumptuary class; but at least the enunciated principle has forced us to examine the critical factor: the coercive aspect rather than any question of physical or psychological harm. The right of humans to run considerable risks (of mental and/or physical damage or even messy and violent demise) in the pursuit of

The possibility of there being a place where everyone's head is at this point of understanding and appreciating nature seems far too distant.

Rebeca Alicia Lopez
Merrill UCSC

How can a utopia be established? First it must be distinguished between wishful thinking and reality, for it has been said that unless a man's programs, theories, methods, etc., correspond with the objective reality, that is, the laws of the external world, man will fail in his endeavor. It has also been said that failure is the mother of success. . .

Sherwin L. Forté
B-21899 Soledad

Karlene's Journal (cont'd.)

for the inmates. He offers us a lot of "guidelines." He creates so much tension. "Be judicious in forming romantic attachments." There are, I know, feelings that prisons should not exist—they should be burned down. But this class is to study utopian societies—it is not set up for political reasons. I don't believe that the North Facility can become a university. But we can make contacts to bring education into this place to give men a better shot at the outside.

Francisco: I'm outraged by your moralizing. We're all students. Some of the limits you put on us are questionable. I *have* definite political biases. Some of the questions cannot be ignored.

The tension in the room has increased. After Donnelly leaves, Ralph tries to get things going again, but the room is very quiet. After a dynamic morning, suddenly it's tense and quiet. Francisco starts talking about the "dirty, fucking minds" here.

Ruben: Sure—people like that are around. You can't let yourself get so upset about it. Don't give it too much attention.

Ralph comments on the problems he has encountered in getting this class passed through the prison administration. His intent is to validate the prison. He is totally opposed to the prison system. He would like to get them all out. But he would be very upset if anything we were to say would cause this class to be cancelled. "If you think this kind of example of prison oppression is intolerable and if you can't take it, perhaps you should not be in this class."

Arthur's Journal (cont'd.)

pleasure is well established. It will be defended—often violently—by such diverse, and often painfully conservative creatures as duck hunters, scuba divers, parachutists, sportscar buffs, and even those peculiar characters who bend F-51s around pylons.

The rationale that has been developed over the years to justify the existence of prisons has been placed into four basic categories by Prof. John Isbister: rehabilitation; deterrence; prevention; punishment. The only one of these four goals that is being fulfilled is that of punishment. Prison is a form of punishment that exists rather than flogging, drawing and quartering, burning at the stake, breaking at the wheel, stocks and more extreme forms of bodily mutilation because on the surface it appears to be a neat, humane, methodical way in which to remove "social offenders" from the public view. All of the other methods which have been used throughout the history of this country do not correspond as well with the technological trends toward efficiency and mass production which exist today.

Gary Pernell
College V UCSC

Karlene's Journal (cont'd.)

Francisco: I will not put up with being treated like a child. I won't be placated. I had to say what was on my mind.

Arthur: We get a vicarious pleasure from his comments—over-reaction by students may have a cathartic value. I wish Francisco had over-reacted more than he did.

Richard: Come on—we deal with it every day. It's not a big thing. We can handle it, and deal with it. If someone walks in, just be cool. We are all over-reacting to this. What else can happen to us, we're here.

Theodore: I see these guys all the time. If I want to say something, I can say it. They can throw me in the hole, ok?

We began to talk again—about the distinction between psychic freedom and physical liberty. Sherwin wants a society based on objective philosophy: "If a drug can be shown scientifically to be positive in its effects, let it be." Much disagreement about who should decide.

Roberto: Let the dope fiends have their own dope city; let 'em shoot up all day. Let 'em OD if they like.

The utopian idea is basically white and as I see it, does not relate to Blacks.

Plezena Shack
Merrill UCSC

Wednesday, April 14, 1971 (Second Meeting)

Having had the temerity to ask for a road map showing the route from the "brainstorming" sessions of the first meeting to the construction of a "New California" along utopian lines, I should be summarily ordered to furnish my first-cut version of such a map. Here it is: I don't like it much but it gives me a vague sense of what we may be striving toward.

Karlene's Journal (cont'd.)

The sign on the wall:

Inmates are not permitted to: receive or use chewing gum; sign anything during visits without permission of the visiting officer; operate vending machines at any time. Visitors are not permitted to give or show anything to an inmate without permission.

The chairs in the visiting room are not to be moved to suit the individual visitor or to be moved closer or placed beside the inmate's chair.

Failure to comply with these rules may be cause for the suspension of visiting privileges.

Suddenly the guard is in the room, jangling his keys at us. There's a spontaneous exchange of the movement handclasp. We smile tentatively at one another, repeating our names, with the guards impatiently shuttling us off, we say goodbye—until next meeting.

Wednesday, April 14, 1971 (Second Meeting)

If we are to discuss what might be, we first need to talk about what is, so the bulk of the morning is given to a discussion of American institutions. Ben and Francisco remind us that our purpose is not to reform the existing institutions but rather to examine the alternative social systems for the meeting of human needs, as outlined at the last meeting.

Arthur's Journal (cont'd.)

Early Brainstorming Sessions
Assorted Bullshit and
Unclassified Notions

Human needs	Major ills of Current Society
Entities which fulfill these human needs	Present institutions and their failings
Fictional models of Utopian Societies	Fictional models of anti-utopias
Attempts at establishing utopian colonies, etc.	Characteristics of anti-utopia and things to avoid like plague

Assumptions and Ground Rules
Major Goals of Utopian Society
Structure and Parameters to
Achieve Goals
Utopian Model of "New California"

I think I split the path of intellectual endeavor into two branches out of habit, acquired during years in the aerospace business, strategic weapons division. Every time we studied, analyzed, or proposed an offensive weapon system, we also examined the potential, possible, and conceptual defense systems someone might develop to counter our threat. The reverse was also done if the initial study was for a strategic defense system. It turned out, in fact, that all efforts were more or less symmetric, in offensive-defensive, whatever

Karlene's Journal (cont'd.)

In the afternoon, at our request, Ralph lays out an historical context—the philosophical/economical foundations on which the country is formed and from which the institutions followed as a response to the State's definition of social order, e.g., the Puritan Ethic of individuality and competition as leading to the acquisition of wealth and the formation of monopolies (institutions evolved to meet needs and answer crises). Polarizations develop and the search continues. Institutions changing with/reacting-to crises.

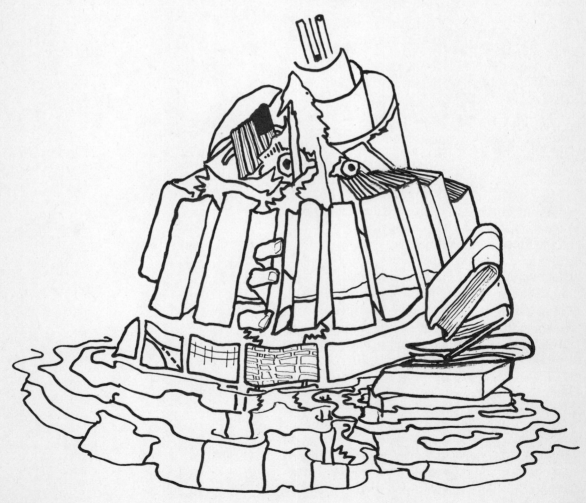

Arthur's Journal (cont'd.)

the initial viewpoint. Intimate familiarity with the wrong way may help find the right. Besides the literature of anti-utopia is fascinating (like Huxley, *Brave New World; Brave New World Revisited;* Wylie, *Generation of Vipers;* Orwell, *1984.*

A number of points were emphasized in the discussion [led by Ralph] of the area outlined [American institutions]. The first had to do with the aristocratic, propertied (and obviously racially absolutely uniformly WASP) and culturally Northern European bias of the "Founding Fathers," who knew long before Orwell that, while all animals are equal, some animals are more equal than others. The second had to do with the origin of the word "penitentiary" and the Friends' pioneering idea of locking up incommunicado evil-doers so that they might contemplate, to the inevitable betterment of their immortal souls, their sins, thereby achieving a mood of penitence— hence the abominable euphemism for their cages. I wonder if it was a Quaker, or merely a sadistic civil servant, who invented the appellation "adjustment center" for what convicts, with characteristic candor, simply call "the hole." The last point I remember being emphasized was that many of our institutions often survived long after the engendering crises had passed and indeed been forgotten.

I'd like to know a bit more about the Puritan Ethic. Is it more than variations on the theme that "suffering equals virtue; pleasure equals sin?" This is the formula that considers "work" to be virtuous, quite apart from the intrinsic usefulness of the work itself. Observe that in the view of the traditional Puritan (and the contemporary Fundamentalist), a specific activity done under duress as a vocation, is virtuous; done voluntarily as a recreation, is either morally neutral or a positive vice. As perverted a concept as was ever exhumed from the graveyard of human rationality.

Individual rehabilitation focusing on the negative act and neglecting the origin of the act can never provide a thorough understanding of the reasons for that action . . . a person cannot be rehabilitated until his original condition (that of habilitation) is not one which by the nature of its existence needs to be rehabilitated.

Gary Pernell
College V UCSC

The constitution has been so pushed out of shape and been changed so much that it don't mean nothing to nobody, even the people who work for the constitution: police, judges, lawyers, etc. This is my response to all American institutions: they just don't have meaning any longer.

Courtney Cain
B-26494 Soledad

Arthur's Journal (cont'd.)

My hackles rise at the issue of individuality. A bullshit shuck; a cruel deception. American individuality means nothing more than the invention of a new way to cheat and exploit. Individuality carried to the incautious extreme of questioning an established principle or goal is rewarded with a truncheon. I level this accusation at two centuries of American society, from Cotton Mather to Billy Graham; from James Madison to John Mitchell. It is one of the most consistent of American phenomena, to tolerate the kind of emasculated individuality that threatens nothing. The kind of individuality provided for by the nation's founders and tolerated by American society at large is analogous to the company union—it is there to pre-empt a legitimate equivalent, to usurp the role of genuine—and hence potentially threatening—individuality. Consider a case in point, the fates of two American purveyors of humor. The first, Bob Hope, court jester to the WASPs, who amuses Middle America by selling it back its own dismal jokes of its lodges and locker rooms. He is a study in averages, in uniform mediocrity; he rates exactly zero in individuality. The second, Lenny Bruce, a unique human being, a true individual, an astonishing talent. America has made Bob Hope very rich, and Lenny Bruce very dead. End of polemic.

It is drummed into every young American male (and probably into many females) that they must become "leaders"—of what, it is unnecessary to specify, but a leader each nipper must become, lest he disgrace his parents and establish himself as a failure and an ingrate. And a "leader" is exactly a possessor of power. "Become a leader" means "acquire power over your fellow man." This may well mean pure power for its own sake—the pious disclaimers of financial motivation are not *invariably* false. The most accurate and chilling description of the nature and use of pure

The elimination or reduction of most institutions can be done through education. This country does not educate but rather brainwashes students. If students were educated properly, presented both sides of the story, then they could chose right from wrong.

Zena Shack
Merrill UCSC

In demanding change, this has been answered in forms from psychic invasion of a person's mind with propaganda to pacifiers such as civil rights which are of no benefit to the poor. To enforce this psychic invasion of the mind they have employed every means available to them, from TV, in early childhood, to institutions and mechanization.

Ruben Gonzales
B-28988 Soledad

From what I read of Huxley's *Island* he seems to me to be a man who was looking for a way to find a utopian society that he couldn't find, so he thought up one out of his mind and wrote of an imaginary utopian society of the kind he would like to live in. It seems he wanted to have peace and a united society and in order to get this point across to the people of the world he started writing about this utopian society. I think he wanted to live in this society, but he also knew that there would never be an island like this and that's why he wrote the book *Island* the way he did.

Courtney Cain
B-26494 Soledad

Arthur's Journal (cont'd.)

power I know is O'Brien's recitation to Winston Smith, at the end of *1984,* of the reasons the Party seeks and maintains its tolaritarian hold on its subjects. I don't have the statement handy to quote but I recall it ends with: "If you want a picture of the future, imagine a boot stamping in a human face—forever."

Huxley and *Island*

Island, is, of course, advocacy masquerading as fiction, in the best tradition of G. B. Shaw, the lecturer masquerading as dramatist. This is not intended in a pejorative sense; unlike Nabokov, I have no specific aversion to didactic literature. And the course is Politics 190c, not English Lit xyz. Huxley is a craftsman of the first order, so the masquerade comes off pretty well; we enjoy the narrative while absorbing the lesson. The literary purpose of Will Farnaby is clear: an unenlightened, pre-psychedelic Anglo-American man, he is tortured by enough typical contemporary problems to be curious about Palanese solutions; his curiosity (which might otherwise seem a trifle strained) is conveniently justified by making him a reporter. So hung-up, uncomprehending Contemporary Western man gets a real-life illustrated lecture from the expanded consciousness of enlightened, psychedelicised, quasi-Eastern Modern Primitive, and the reader gets to go along. We can forgive Mr. Farnaby for being a bit one-dimensional; he is really only a sounding board (perhaps I should therefore deem him two-dimensional). What humanity he displays is largely through his hang-ups; they are so damned familiar. Mr. Farnaby is us, sort of; perhaps he is also that empuly urbane writer who once concerned himself with the posturings of the British week-end-at-the-country-place set in works like *Antic Hay.*

The only people who write down their utopian dreams are persons who worry about the system: but the people can be so very unreal. It's the real people I love and grieve for—the newer better world should be for them.

Mona Burns
College V UCSC

Arthur's Journal (cont'd.)

Despite the temptation to focus on *Island* as literature and Huxley as author, it is precisely with the didactic aspects of the book that we are concerned. I have called Huxley a "psychedelic utopian"; and I will reassure the assembled Cleaver fans that by this I mean that Huxley advocates a path to utopia that involves psychedelics, *not* that he envisions utopia as the Land of the Perpetually Stoned. He may in fact favor this latter view, but it is not the position taken in *Island*.

What, precisely, is a psychedelic utopian as opposed, say, to a political one? A political utopian, in my definition, is one who focuses on alteration of social and political institutions, as the way to utopia. Provide ideal institutions, he proclaims, and man will function optimally within their framework, adapting himself to them as necessary. A psychedelic utopian takes the reverse view. Change human nature, he says, into something more or less ideal, and appropriate changes in man's institutions will follow. An adjunct belief is the theory that, without fundamental change in human nature, a utopian society, or even an appreciable change for the better in human institutions, is impossible. With this despairing conclusion I am in perfect agreement.

A fundamental change in human nature— that is a tall order. What can be found that is sufficiently powerful to convert the subhuman warmasters with their chained Einsteins into beings fit to occupy an earthly semi-paradise? Of course. Dope; *moksha*-medicine. Properly (strong) psychedelics. That is the lesson of *Island*.

I think there may be some argument on this point. First, it is currently fashionable in militant third-world circles to reject drugs as a honky trick to lull the steam out of the revolution (aggravated by a tendency of people who are stoned to giggle at most leftist dialectic). The second argument is more difficult:

Such emphasis in Huxley's interpretation of a utopia is placed on the integration of mind and body, nature and science, the idea of incorporating "all possible fronts." In contrast, our society has its foundations rooted firmly in a dualistic nature—while technology is pedestaled and worshipped, our spirtuality is in a state of degeneration and moral decay.

Ranko Yamada
Merrill UCSC

Arthur's Journal (cont'd.)

I simply cannot believe that anyone who has not experienced the . . . *moksha*-state could take seriously the notion of a chemically induced permanent and profound improvement in human potential. *Island* will strike the psychedelically virginal as a naive and visionary work, or perhaps as parable (maybe the moksha-medicine equals Eucharist or the Thoughts of Chairman Mao); only the initiates will recognize that its proposals are meant to be taken more or less literally. In view of their apparent extravagance—the direct descendent of the *moksha*-experience—how could it be otherwise? There may, in our class, be a sort of unbridgeable dichotomy in this regard.

What comments can be ventured on the validity of the psychedelic utopian hypothesis? The portion of the hypothesis that avers that any major change for the better in human existence must be preceded by a fundamental change in human nature seems to be established beyond dispute. Witness four thousand grim years of history. Less indisputable is the postulate that psychedelic drugs offer a method for producing the requisite change in human potential (here potential is more accurate than "nature": the most enthusiastic proponent of psychedelics could hardly claim for them the property of compelling human virtue, at best they make the acquisition of virtues an easier process). Advocates of this postulate may cite Monterey and Woodstock, but they must account for Altamont; they may cite Castalia (on the Hitchcock property in Duchess County, New York) but they must account for Spahn Ranch. A lot of turgid water has flowed under the bridge since 1962. The subject of the values and dangers of psychedelics has been emotionally charged since the beginning to an unprecedented degree; when it became politically profitable along about 1964, to damn drugs as the chemical incarnation of Satan, the last vestiges of rational discourse (and

Arthur's Journal (cont'd.)

effectively all objective scientific research) vanished. The environment since 1967, has been one in which the official sanction is given to the most savage and irrational oppression of anything even hinting at psychedelics; they are today's version of Cotton Mather's witches. In such an environment I suggest that it is impossible to conduct a meaningful investigation into the merits of psychedelics; it is nearly impossible to conduct a rational discussion based on the data available to date. We are drowned in a tsunami of anti-dope propaganda. It fills the pages of newspapers and magazines; it is vomited unceasingly from the tube; it booms from countless pulpits; it is the backbone of every curriculum and the sturdiest plank in every platform. Most of it is unadulterated crap. But it is as abhorrent scientifically speaking, to reject it all out of hand as it would be to accept it because it came from a divinely inspired source—Art Linkletter. We may hold our private opinions (as I do), but we are more or less prohibited from any objective research until the hysteria abates.

The Family and Its Relation
to Utopian Societies

No comment—for once.

The mother is supposed to be the symbol of love, warmth, and understanding, yet in many instances her own children are afraid to communicate with her. A self-induced fear together with misconceptions on the part of both parents. To add further to the problem, society as a whole along with all their technology, mass media, television, and commercialization, are fighting one another for the privilege of instructing children as to what's right and wrong. All these things further reduce father, mother roles to absolute oblivion. They are not qualified to compete against these odds. And thereby fail to establish any real kind of meaningful relationship between themselves, but most importantly, with their children.

Ruben Gonzales
B-28988 Soledad

As a *Chicano* I cannot blame my parents for the ways I was raised, simply because we all suffered together and went through our times of darkness together. What brought us together was the warmth of trying to console each other that things would change. So in this sense we the *Chicanos* were brought together while others were separating themselves.

Ruben Reyna
B-21734 Soledad

Arthur's Journal (cont'd.)

Monday, April 19, 1971 (Third Meeting)

A visiting professor from UCSC lectured on early utopian literature and colonies. The import seemed to be this: the experiments in utopian communes, or at least in special-purpose communes which might have seemed more or less utopian to their members, commenced in the U.S.A. in the mid-nineteenth century. The salient example of one that was fairly large and sufficiently durable to last

The socialization of infants . . . I really believe it is the single vital function left to the nuclear family now and in the foreseeable future . . . in my own utopia, "school" would begin at about six months. The state might require attendance to protect the child against his parents' tendency to isolate him and the state should provide some of the materials. Little else would resemble the present nurseries or preschools. Such an infant school would be comprised of about three families who would simply get their children together a couple times a week. The group size would increase as the child got older. The families would spend quite a bit of time together, discussing their children or anything else as well. The idea that only "professionals" are able to teach is a myth. Parents teach children a host of complicated things before they are five years old and could very likely teach them after this age just as well.

Mona Burns
College V UCSC

Arthur's Journal (cont'd.)

about thirty years was the 1846 Oneida, New
York, community (later the "Community
Plate" people). Their major source of income
was from the manufacture and sale of a super-
ior proprietary line of animal traps. The world,
it seems, beat a path to Oneida. The community was religious in basis (although upholding,
it would appear, a satisfactorily flexible interpretation regarding the commandment about
killing), and sent its sons to Yale. It got back
atheists, which is more than it deserved; a community devoted to the production of animal
traps should have gotten back William F.
Buckley.

In the latter part of the nineteenth century,
the experimental communes apparently attracted mostly out-of-work tradesmen, arti-
sans, and the like. The working class make-up
of these communes made them forebearers of
the labor movement, the theoretical and intellectual efforts in the direction of utopia seem
to have found more outlet in literature than in
experiment. After the considerable financial
success of the anonymously published *Looking
Backward*, by one Edward Bellamy, there was
a flurry of utopian fiction purveyed by persons
whose concern for mankind's future was at
least matched by an equal concern for their
own present. Apparently the market soon became saturated for the output of utopian fiction quickly settled down to a small, desul-
tory trickle.

The notion was batted around that isolated
primitive societies (historical and modern
alike) could be considered utopian, at least to
a degree. To a negligible degree, I suggest. An
unromanticized look at the life of most prim-
itives reveals ignorance, fear, squalor, disease,
pain, oppression, and early death—the last item
perhaps a benefit in view of the prevalence of
the others. There is no room in utopia for
hookworm, and rodents dining on infants.

I believe a utopian society has existed in America! The Indians, the
first known natives of this country,
lived and survived in a very utopian
sense. Not until the . . . exploitation
of the "European monster" did the
Indian know oppression—in all forms.

Michael Lee
B-24542-A Soledad

I figure we're all in this mess, even though some of us had a bigger hand in making it than others, and we should all stick it out until some good comes of it.

Debra Walton
Merrill UCSC

The burning commitment at the altar of every utopia is the conviction that men can live in community, define their goals and reach them without rising up to destroy each other. And we do hold things in common, not the least of them our urge to meet on this common ground. So the question may be asked, if it can be done, why can't we do it? Further, if we can't, who can?

Mona Burns
College V UCSC

Arthur's Journal (cont'd.)

Afternoon

The sub-group discussions were to focus on what I have called the difference in approach separating the political utopians from the psychedelic ones. At our table, Mike Rotkin [a visiting graduate student from UCSC] for the political, me for the psychedelic (this is something of an oversimplification; the session was a blend of discussion and advocacy). We examined several major (apparent) changes in human institutions to see if, as in the political utopian view, they wrought a corresponding change in human behavior or human nature, whatever that might mean. Samples: a transplant from *barrio* to prosperous suburbia; the abolition of slavery in the United States; the Russian Revolution; the Cuban Revolution. Some interesting conclusions arose. In the case of the *barrio* transplant (where the change of institutions was to be effected by moving the subject into an entirely different environment), the conclusion seemed to be that, because somehow the change was not fundamental, the subject would adapt without really changing in any significant way. In the case of the abolition of slavery, it was suggested that economic enslavement replaced legal and political slavery, and that the change in institutions was mostly on paper; this was offered as the reason that racial attitudes and antagonisms enjoyed so little benefit from the eradication of Black slavery as an institution. The Russian Revolution was noted by Mike as a point for the psychedelic view: a major change in institutions produced no discernable improvement in the generally miserable behavior of the Russians as regards political oppression, elitism, the dictatorial concentration of absolute power, etc. Finally, it was generally acknowledged that the Cubans are currently too busy getting their economy in shape, in the face of relentless hostility from their former

Certain individuals have certain fears and dislikes toward each of these issues—politics and drugs—and I know we should evaluate them more thoroughly. But we must keep in mind that in order to reach a certain structure about what utopia is and how we can reach our own utopian society, we need to evaluate other issues as well. For instance: education, the court system, and economics.

Theodore Martinez
B-24564 Soledad

Arthur's Journal (cont'd.)

commercial partner, Uncle Sam, to put much effort into modifying their institutions along utopian lines; Cuba remains, therefore, an open issue.

Experiments in psychedelic utopias were discussed less—they, of course, have been on a smaller scale than the political operations mentioned above. Chicho [Pedro] reported that he had once been part of a successful music and drug commune in the Haight; Mike had participated in a psychedelic-based commune that was a dismal flop, and a mostly political-oriented group that was a modest success. I refrained then, as I will at this point, from introducing my own experiences into the argument (there may be time for this later). The discussion closed with Mike's question as to what specific improvements in character or behavior might be expected to be the general consequence of a program of psychedelic exploration. I suggested a decline in conspicuous overconsumption as an example. This was countered with the spectacle of the plastic hippie, alighting from a gleaming GTO wearing $45 beads. Well, such creatures certainly exist, and some of them have actually ingested real psychedelics (a large number have not, despite their claims and beliefs). But psychedelics are catalysts; the rest of the reaction—"set and setting"—is critical in determining the ultimate effect. I would suggest that a tiny percentage of the apparitions described have undergone the kind of *moksha*-experience described by Huxley. I would further add that a failure percentage—even a sizeable one—would not necessarily mean that psychedelics are not a valuable agent for the betterment of human behavior; all the other agents I can think of have a failure percentage of one hundred. I will close by observing that the contest in our sub-group ended as a sort of draw—but I retain my predeliction.

There seems to be a sense of confusion—as individuals we are becoming in tune with our own concepts of utopia: but we struggle for some kind of concensus in order that we might "work together." However, after Dr. Guzman explained what was happening—"Just float with the material, and let it develop its relevance . . . " I am better able to deal with it. American institutions have been a hypocritical collection of laws, mores, and dreams which are all relative—meaning different things at different times to different people in different places.

Richard Risher
B-21915 Soledad

I strongly disagree with the students who feel there is only one approach to creating a utopian society. Man is a tremendously diverse animal and one man's answer is just that: one man's answer. Since we must all eventually live our lives according to our individual beliefs, we must be willing to sacrifice in certain areas for the common good. If we approach social problems from only one side we are taking the blind approach. There is a real prison system which keeps us from achieving an ideal social order and this prison is the confines of our own minds. Some men are imprisoned with notions of wealth and power: others want only to retreat from the social order and its chaotic and cruel institutions. In order to free ourselves from a socially restrictive society, we must transcend that society. The limitations of our intellect are reflected in those who speak of reform in society. To challenge concepts in society would be to free ourselves from restrictive intellectual bonds. Unless we develop a consciousness for the needs of others we will stay imprisoned within ourselves. We are all to one extent or another products of the institutions which have controlled our lives and conditioned us to respond in certain acceptable patterns. Until we challenge the very foundations of our societal institutions we cannot hope to escape the prison-like confines of our political environment. Only thus can we escape the prison of our minds.

Ben Dunn
Merrill UCSC

Karlene's Journal (cont'd.)

Wednesday, April 21, 1971 (Fourth Meeting)

Ruben: The literature hardly relates to me; it fails to deal with my experience, the here and now.

Ben: We don't want to just reform institutions; we need to define them in terms of their usefulness or outmodedness and maybe eliminate some of them.

Arthur's Journal (cont'd.)

Wednesday, April 21, 1971 (Fourth Meeting)

Chaos. I am quoted by Sherwin as having advocated a society in which everyone is stoned into complete immobility. This is precisely what I have been at some pains not to advocate. I don't mind being misquoted; what saddens me is that any position repeatedly stated with agonizing efforts at clarity, is misunderstood. There is a distinct tendency not to listen, particularly in the full group, and in Sherwin's case, I have a feeling I am confronted by Black dogma: dope is a crackah trick to divert the revolutionary drive of the Black man into unproductive channels. Goddamnit, smack may be that to a small degree when it is tolerated in the Inner City; but this is not what I'm talking about, nor Huxley, nor Dr. Leary, who has been "exposed" by the BPP. Exposed as *what* for heaven's sake? As a doper? That hardly constitutes a revelation. If anything, the exposure was the other way around. Leary's inane revolutionary posturings, from his shaky Algerian beachhead under Eldridge's guns is patently in payment for his liberation and sanctuary, and renders suspect any claims the militants might make for their altruism and brotherhood-in-adversity in the Leary matter. They sprung him to add his forensic talents to their shabby stable of propagandists, and I suspect he will be in some peril when his usefulness in that role is ended.

A religion capable of fitting within a utopia must be fluid and vulnerable to change. Rather than a rigid standard meant to gain acceptance by an all-powerful god, it would be a philosophy, an understanding. Possibly a few people would be placed as exemplary figures, but it would be clear that in essence they are no more than anyone else.

Ranko Yamada
Merrill UCSC

Karlene's Journal (cont'd.)

Richard: Any platform for change is an utopian endeavor.

Theodore: Get rid of drugs in utopia, except grass.

Courtney: The church is used as a propagandizing tool of the state—it's a pacifier like drugs.

Francisco: Primitive societies, as opposed to those dominated by a Calvinistic ethos, emphasize the natural order with religion permeating nature.

Sherwin: As man has developed his rational faculties, he has had less need for religion as an explanation for misfortune.

Theodore: Restore religion but get rid of false idols with religion as a pacifier of the disadvantaged.

Ruben: It's courting disaster to bring in Russian communists (like Fidel did)—I'm turned off to Cuba as a model for revolutionary change.

Key question raised, discussed, unresolved; e.g., Is life improved by changing the institutions and trusting human nature to exert its natural goodness? Or do we strive to change human character and then expect better institutions to evolve?

Paths to Utopia

Psychedelia (dystopians)	Utopia	Politics (utopians)
subjective	dialetics	objective

Arthur's Journal (cont'd.)

Progress. Some of the issues, class attitudes, and approaches to the overall task of the class are crystallizing. I will try to record my impressions here. Despite any suspicions the reader might entertain, I neither pack a luger nor affect a monocle.

By far the most significant thing to come out of the last two classes is the transformation intact, of the political versus psychedelic approach dichotomy into racial divergence. The (nearly?) unanimous view of the Black members of the class (Soledad and Santa Cruz branches alike) appears to be the political one. The honkies favor, rather less unswervingly, the psychedelic approach; the Chicano/Oriental faction is ambiguous. Readers of the underground press will recognize the existence of a very similar situation throughout the "movement." This fracturing has proven no more amenable to repair in class than in the national arena. We are here not so much concerned with analyzing the sources of this breach than with its effects on the course of study of utopian societies in a multi-racial class. Since we can't heal the breach, we more or less decided to incorporate it into the subject matter of the course. To be explicit the written contributions of the class members dealing with approaches to, and the structure of, utopian societies, will be examined to determine what characteristics display a clear-cut racial correlation. The nature and degree of this correlation may be considered one of the study results.

The issue of the political versus psychedelic view of the road to utopia has an analog in the expected variation in structure and emphasis of the utopian societies that may be favored by members of the class. Students from racial minorities (who very likely have experienced both disenfranchisement and economic deprivation), tend to view utopia in immediate and

Only when identification with the problem, and with the oppressed, occurs can the person begin to find constructive, effective means. Missionary trips are never welcomed completely even under the most deceptive guise.

Ranko Yamada
Merrill UCSC

Karlene's Journal (cont'd.)

In the afternoon we met in three small groups—without conscious intent everyone divided up into primarily ethnic groups. Five Caucasians and Francisco are in my group. Sherwin who had begun talking with me several times earlier, said he thought I should be in his "political group," which was mostly Black. He said there was already a strong political activity in the making with a program written up—wanted to present it to the group—a small group with solidarity. Not wanting to abandon the whites—by far the smallest and most vulnerable-looking group—I said I'd be a floater and went back. We discussed the ethnic division. Arthur and Don [a prisoner transferred from Soledad before the course was completed] talked about the dominance of ethnic groups over whites within the prison.

Don: We need "white power," too. All the other guys in other ethnic groups can organize themselves. Whites can't.

Arthur: Divide and conquer.

We talked about power and leadership—how minorities and new leftists advocate a political solution that substitutes one regime for another. Same old problem—sad history of revolution. They want to kill the king and take over the throne. Why not get rid of the throne? Keep down the size of the community. Decentralize. Don is concerned about being "ruled" by anybody. Ben appeals to him to proceed with his individualistic trip but to be sensitive to the needs and common interests within the group.

Arthur's Journal (cont'd.)

practical terms, generally within a political and economic context. The "white" students—children of relative affluence and racially indistinguishable from the occupants of the seats of power—can afford a visionary view, tending to stress the intangibles of an idealized human existence. No attempt will be made in the class to reconcile or coalesce these variations in viewpoints—it is sufficient to recognize them and have a passable understanding of their origins. The class is in fact partly tutorial and partly in way of research; in the latter category, it may provide a revealing picture of the influence of ethnic and socio-economic background on a human being's notion of the ideal environment for his species.

The belief in the white man's burden has its counterpart in "white liberals" who feel a strong sense of helping the "disadvantaged, unfortunate, culturally deprived" people of color to find a better life. These modern-day missionaries are repulsive in the fact that their racism is disguised in supposed "higher" feelings of humanity. Liberal paternalism is reflected not only in individual attitudes but in the procedures and policies of institutions such as the welfare system and most "war on poverty" efforts.

Ranko Yamada
Merrill UCSC

Like everyone dedicated to radical change, I find the burden of proof resting squarely on my shoulders. "Nowhere to run, nowhere to hide . . . " If I feel that the way people, the way I live to be lacking—isn't it my duty to propose something concrete to accompany the destruction I pledge to sow? I must know what it is I want and how, then "want" will come about. I have fulfilled nothing—no part of my revolutionary duty—in merely lighting the fuse. I must know the existing horror, I must allow its knowledge to ache in my heart. Beyond the pain, I must construct a new reality—a wholeness that will not feel the need to hide itself. An outfront, wrapped-tight righteous new way that depends on honesty and draws its sustenance from brother-sisterhood.

Deirdre Stone
Cowell UCSC

Karlene's Journal (cont'd.)

When we come back together with the whole group, the conflict proceeds between pragmatists who don't want to escape into a religion/drug-induced state of bliss. ("There's work to be done.") and those who endorse change through mind-altering transformation. Francisco mentions the Berkeley election which harnessed the hippie-dropout-stoners to elect a radical slate of councilmen.

Sherwin: For peace and harmony there is only one utopia; we need everyone's energy and we can't have dead escapists.

Don: We're all in this together. It comes back to individualism versus collectivity.

Theodore: We need to reflect 100% on the existing system if we are to think in utopian terms.

Arthur (asks Sherwin): Who has done more to increase social awareness? Tim Leary or Huey Newton?

[Zena gets *mad*.]

Sherwin: They represent different groups.

Arthur: Precisely; Newton wants concrete changes; Leary has affected things. He called attention to the problems and suggested solutions. Both he and Newton are propagandists—Leary has reached ten times more people than Newton.

Francisco: He's telling the middle class to drop out . . . they have no obvious reason to do that . . . but when they get busted for acid they are in the process of becoming politicized.

Arthur's Journal (cont'd.)

A discussion of power (in the social or political sense) transpired without any very definite conclusions arising. Some issues worth noting were raised. It was agreed that a utopian society by anyone's definition should be minimally coercive toward its members. Yet anything that could conceivably be referred to as a society must have power, when all else fails, for compelling obedience to its rules. Who in utopia may be trusted as the repository of this power? What will prevent this agency, since it is ultimately answerable to nothing save itself, from embarking on the historical course of cancerous enlargement for its own ends? In the creation of a utopian society, how can the classical failures of the past revolutions—the replacement of one tyranny by another—be avoided? These questions have been mentioned but, of course, not answered with certainty short of successful practice. But they remain critical, and fascinating; subjects for further investigation.

One of the basic assumptions is that aggression among people is the result of poor tolerance for ordinary frustrations and learned competitiveness. It follows that if they can learn to cope with frustrations and to live without competing for property or prestige, people will not display aggression. Although this was probably accepted generally in the late 40's, it has been opened again to question in the 60's by a variety of sociologists, biologists, and anthropologists who claim that aggression is to some extent innate and related to the presumably innate aggressive behavior of other primates. Clearly if this were the case, no amount of training would completely rid the community of the threat of aggression and some means to deal with it would become necessary almost immediately. Even if aggression and competitiveness could be trained away; do they in fact account for a substantial part of the motivation which accomplishes the work of society? I am inclined to agree that they do.

Mona Burns
College V UCSC

In this white American society, class-ification, similar to the caste system in India, is in operation: upper, middle, and lower class with the majority of Blacks below the lower class. Because of this, I feel a driving rage to eliminate the subjects responsible.

Phillip Jacobs
B-21434-A Soledad

When asked if I'm involved in the revolution, I answer, "I am the revolution." When someone forces me to do things his way, he's violating my personal code and that's where I revolt. The revolution has been started but it hasn't gotten out of mind level. We may need a blood spill. A spark to ignite it. Where there's a thunderstorm, one doesn't need a barometer to predict the weather. There are rebels without cause. In our *barrios* these rebels are called *los batos locos* (crazy dudes) or plainly somebody that just don't give a big fuck. This dude has been ready since 1954-55. He's just a rebel without a cause. But his heart tells him there's something wrong and that's cause enough. Just the simple reasons for not knowing.

Ruben Reyna
B-21734 Soledad

In a true revolution, change cannot be accomplished without some bloodshed. And every drop of blood soaked up by the soil serves as an offering for the redemption of the exploited and oppressed people wherever they may be. And for every *carnal* that falls there must be a thousand outstretched hands ready to pick up his weapon in order to carry on the fight. Others, however, feel that the pen is mightier than the sword and thus seek knowledge. Yes, *carnales*, violence is a necessity, but why not give the thinkers and knowledge seekers a chance?

Ruben Gonzales
B-28988 Soledad

I'm a social reject and an active non-conformist and I've given the best years of my life to the prison and military service of this sick American government. And it's funny to realize that upon my "release" I'm just going to an outside prison. My life here is controlled, but upon my return only a few so-called rights will be restored. I feel that only when bullets start to flow by blacks, browns, yellows and poor whites, can any type of utopia be reached. Bullets are the only things our capitalistic madmen can comprehend. The mad dogs now in power are concerned only about the profits lining their pockets. Capitalism, socialism, communism all aspire to the same end, differing only in the methods used. The hardships suffered by so many people are absurd. Wealth of this country, earned by the work of countless minorities, should be used to better the conditions—economic and educational—for everyone.

Phillip Jacobs
B-21434-A Soledad

Arthur's Journal (cont'd.)

Like *Island, Walden Two* is advocacy disguised as fiction—thinly disguised. Skinner's literary craftsmanship is of a rather lower order than Huxley's, and *Walden Two* is an uneven and frequently clumsy effort.

Where does Skinner fall with respect to our raging political versus psychedelic division? Some preliminary discussion with other class members has turned up the interesting notion that he is in the political camp. This seems to be related to the opinion that Skinner is in some way "practical" as compared to Huxley, who is dismissed as visionary. Whether or not this is true, I suggest that Skinner is squarely in the psychedelic camp: *Island* has *moksha-*medicine, *Walden Two* has applied behavioral psychology. It is faithful to the principle that

Why does a black or brown man join the armed services? Escape from the compelling and disheartening forces of the environment they're forced to live in; the discontent of educational progress hampered by the unequal distribution of material and scholarships; the prospect of a better life and the opportunity to travel. What are they told after entering? Our main duty is to halt the creeping communism. You respond to this crap, being young and foolish, by a sort of spirit of the corps and patriotism. What do you see in Vietnam? Something strange occurs or your vision goes bad: you seem to see more black and brown people in the front lines than you had expected. The minority becomes the majority at the front. Then you find out that you've been fucked again by the master of deception. You find yourself just a human tool in achieving his master plan—world domination. What happens when you get home? You find your enemy is still the upper and middle class white. And your dues are still as fictional as before you went across the pond. But the seed has been planted for your freedom. You realize the steps necessary to achieve success: armed struggle.

Phillip Jacobs
B-21434-A Soledad

We carry the seed of life but we also carry the germ of destruction, and let's not forget it.

Pedro Chacon
B-8747 Soledad

Arthur's Journal (cont'd.)

a necessary initial step in the formation of a utopian society is some kind of fundamental change in the potential members.

Skinner's place among the psychedelic utopians is secure—an unsurprising tenure for a professor of psychology.

Skinner (often speaking through Frazier) frequently achieves the ridiculous in his earnest efforts to reassure us that everything and everybody in *Walden Two* is meant to function in perfect accord with every conceivable legal and moral precept in postwar America. How Mrs. Grundy would have applauded those delicately segregated decontamination chambers! The *Walden Two* farmhands not only are not going to offend, they by God aren't going to risk turning into voyeurs while being deodorized. True, the postadolescents in *Walden Two* are enabled to gratify their blossoming sexual drives—after they have been thoroughly checked out by the Manager of Marriages. Roll *that* phrase, "the manager of marriages," around your imagination a bit. And (presuming they don't just say the hell with it at some point) after they have duly legalized their nuptial vows they are encouraged to occupy the same room (after an advisory session with the Manager of Fucking?) during the female's "child-bearing years." After that—I think I detect the aroma of that ancient and unlamented Calvinist doctrine that sex, at best tolerable as the necessary technique of procreation, is for any other purpose immoral. The citizens of *Walden Two,* we are asked to believe, find this, and numerous other bric-a-brac, entirely unperturbing. If they do, they must closely resemble those astonishing plastic androids one encounters at decency rallies and in the chorus of the "Up with People" roadshow: clean, *clean, CLEAN,* and if you haul down their knickers, they turn out to be as innocent of genitals as Ken and Barbie.

Although the people of *Walden Two* were governed by a fascist rule "incognito," they were satisfied. The major contradictions that seemed to plague all social beings were resolved, not by the people themselves but by the well advanced technologists. The people had nothing to worry about. All and everything was provided except for certain virtues that push man on to progress—personal incentive, the winner motivation to strive, to reach the goal, to continue to struggle until that certain goal is reached. True the community was productive and progressive—the socialist theory was quite well used—but still I would merely define their commune system as a form of critical-utopian-socialism. They rejected all political action, they wished to attain their goals by peaceful means and they thrived on experiments—large and small. So the freedom that the people of *Walden Two* experienced was not a forced freedom. They were not able to determine their own destiny. They were governed by a dictatorship that they were not aware of.

Michael Lee
B-24542-A Soledad

Politically it can be argued that *Walden Two* has an authoritarian taint, but personally, I think that the people in the book take a more active role in decision-making and take more measures to keep the planners and managers honest than one would think. Even as it stands *Walden* is much more humanitarian than the most democratic of today's exploitative and moribund systems. If I could find a "Walden Two" I would join it.

Sherwin Forté
B-21899 Soledad

I really felt moved when I read about the success of *Walden Two,* almost as if I was part of the pages with its unity. I found only one thing wrong—its community was totally for all whites, which leaves me out. But I still need to keep my desire intact, toward a very rewarding experience which I must admit captivated my interest and moved me a great deal toward an understanding of what utopia really could be like.

Theodore Martinez
B-24564 Soledad

Arthur's Journal (cont'd.)

I have searched *Walden Two* in vain for a suggestion as to why unswerving conformity to the prevailing outside moral codes (in their strictest interpretations) should be necessary in the utopian community (visible conformity to the outside legal codes may be justified on the basis of survival). I am fully aware that this conformity is not induced by force, or the threat of it, and that much of the *Walden* code may be unwritten. This mitigates neither the severity of the code nor the means used to effect compliance with it. An accepted pattern of behavior, carefully planned, exists; adherence to the pattern by the members is induced by forces which, as Frazier points out, are consciously and systematically invoked, and are ultimately more potent than coercion. The prevailing legal and moral codes found in the United States in 1948 were intended to tame a distinctly unreconstructed body politic. It seems inconsistent and unjustified, if the behavioral engineering of Frazier and the other Planners works as advertised, to apply these codes undiluted to the super-citizens of *Walden Two*. Let me offer a specific example. In *Walden Two*, premarital chastity and post-marital fidelity, if not specifically required by rule, are implicitly vigorously sanctioned. I thought I detected an ominous undertone of suggestion that post-marital chastity might be the next step, what with artificial insemination lurking in the shadows of Frazier's visionary closet, but I will accept his disclaimers and let it pass. Now these arcane virtues originated as bastions of the family unit, in an epoch when the feudal state, or the primitive family state, was in constant need of soldiers and slavers and tillers of the soil, and underpopulation was viewed with the alarm aroused by its opposite today. The same applies to sexual jealousy, the alleviation of which might be advanced as an argument for marital fidelity. Sexual jealousy is an acquired rather than

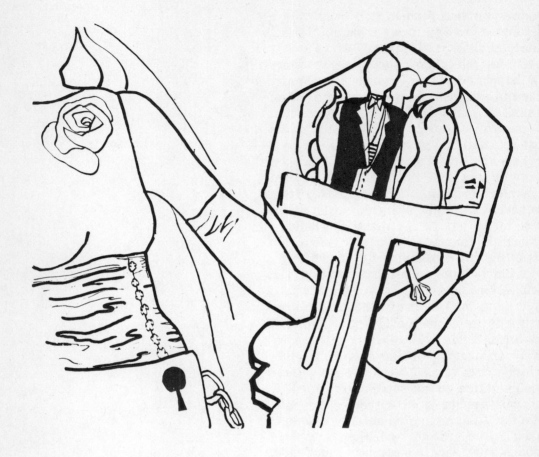

Our moral standards should be optional. The present taboos only invite rebels to violate them. They're bogus and without substantial meaning. For example, women saving their virginity for wedding night . . . how counterfeit can we get?

William Lute
B-25871-B Soledad

Arthur's Journal (cont'd.)

inborn emotion; it is generally advocated as a supposedly cohesive agent in the family structure. It certainly served no other useful purpose, with the conceivable exception of stimulating the commercial well-being of detective agencies and dealers in deadly weapons. When the family no longer serves any of its traditional purposes (breeding, ecclesiastical or military recruitment, education) and indeed has begun to be systematically downgraded in social importance, what is the point in maintaining uncomfortable constraints on human behavior whose sole justification is the preservation of the family? Skinner offers no answer.

It might be argued that the moral constraints of *Walden Two* are not uncomfortable (none of the rules is, if one accepts the notion that behavioral engineering can make anything palatable); but that in itself is no justification for their existence. I cannot believe the sanctioned behavior patterns (at least in some salient departments) are "natural" ones which will blossom in the benign atmosphere of *Walden Two*; nor do I think any amount of applied behavioral psychology likely to alter this state of affairs. Left to his own devices, *homo sapiens* is neither conspicuously chaste nor monagomous, and these shortcomings are so universal a feature of the human landscape that it seems appropriate to deem them rather fundamental human characteristics. In this light, Skinner's utopia cries out in vain for a relaxation of some of the prohibitions which vex the lives of those less fortunate souls outside. Utopian man, behavioral engineering, notwithstanding, should be natural man; but in this regard *Walden Two* seems to be a failure.

It occurs to me that I may be flaying *Walden Two* for a personal idiosyncracy of its author. Skinner may be, in addition to a behaviorist, a four-square prude. One would expect no less from a psychologist. My tendency

Arthur's Journal (cont'd.)

to consider psychologists to be character-
istically somewhat looney is aggravated in
Skinner's case by the personalities of his fictional creations. The characters of *Walden
Two*—particularly Frazier—are mere spokes-
men and adversaries for Skinner's views; as
such they would quite naturally be personi-
fications of their creator to one degree or
another. To a man they are vain, insecure, self-
doubting, neurotics; and Frazier is a sort of
psychotic Stephen Potter, engaged in an endless and badly managed round of one-
upmanship.

I find myself in partial agreement·with the
gentleman called Castle with regard to the
atmosphere of *Walden Two*. Skinner simply
does not offer a believable environment for
unlobotmized humans (and if Frazier's behavioral engineering is lobotomy without the
scalpel, then Castle's most vigorous condemnation is both justified and entirely inadequate). In the early pages of the book, I found
myself recognizing *Walden Two*—it is Soledad
(on a voluntary basis) after a well-financed
cleanup by a pack of liberal club women.

Lest it be concluded that I am utterly
satanic, seeing as how I have opted for dope,
promiscuity, infidelity, and adolescent sexual
perversion, let me observe that my real objec-
tion to the society of *Walden Two* is its absence of color. All the color, all the infinite
variety, has been squeezed out of the life and
the citizens—I keep wanting to call them inmates—of *Walden Two*. They do what they
want to, but their choices are at bottom in-
describably dull. The residents are content but
not, I suggest, affirmatively happy; they are
artsy-craftsy as hell (possibly exhibiting extraordinary skill), but probably not creative; they
display virtuosity but not artistry; they are
(occasionally) sexual but never sensuous; they
enjoy the peace of mind of a ruminant. The
class list of basic human needs includes

So just what is a "perfect society?"
Just a dream in one's mind? A society
in which everyone is free to do as she
or he likes? To do this everyone would
have to be in complete harmony with
each other. This whole discussion is
very complicated to me. Perhaps due
to the fact that I'm now in the state
prison. A prison within a screwed-up
society. A reject to the only society
I've ever been exposed to. When I get
released, it won't be a big thing. Like
I'm not really getting nothing. An outsider might say, "Well, at least you
won't be locked up." But nothing will
be changed if I'm again exposed to a
society that still is run by the same
capitalistic monsters as those who run
the prison system now.

Roberto Arras
B-24050 Soledad

Arthur's Journal (cont'd.)

compelling intangibles like competition (out-
lawed in *Walden Two*) and significant challenge; extraordinary states of consciousness
and mystical experience (non-existent at *Walden Two*); ritual (obsolete at *Walden Two*);
meaningful available variety of life-style (impractical at *Walden Two*). And in the final
analysis it may be that the essence missing
from *Walden Two* is the touch of evil—real
evil, not the sort of schoolboy naughtiness for
which two demerits are accorded. Is it possible
that man, robbed of the opportunity to engage
in the vain, unceasing struggle against a dark
and universal adversary—whose domain, of
course, lies in the depths of his own psyche—
loses at the same time that indefinable internal
fire that the pious call the soul?

As a penalty for being a singularly low
class of prisoner (status being acquired through
a seniority I neither have nor seek), I am forced to occupy a cell located adjacent to the
wing game-and-TV-viewing area. I must, as a
further result of my lowly estate, occupy that
cell much of the time—I am, for example, simply locked up after dinner each evening, a
measure of unquestionable rehabilitation value. The management has thoughtfully provided
extra speakers for the TV audio, one of these
being mounted over the door of my cell. I
thus am favored each evening with 3½ hours
of clearly heard, but unseen television. The inmates favor programs dealing with crime and
violence (I believe there may be other types),
and have an odd predilection, considering
their social condition, for law enforcement
agents as protagonists. Did you know that
Dragnet sometimes plays twice in the same
day? *I* know. A typical program sequence consists of "Dragnet," "High Chapparal" (sheriff
hero), "Ironsides" (policeman hero), and
"Dragnet" again, the series interspersed with
some bilious "variety." A volume control setting of 10 out of a possible 10 is standard, in

Arthur's Journal (cont'd.)

order that the TV may be heard over the ambient conversation, which is in turn carried on
in shouts so that they may be heard over the
ambient TV. The result, which penetrates my
cubicle despite improvised newspaper sound-
proofing, is very loud and weirdly fragmented.
I will try to recreate a little of it, in dramatic
form:

Anonymous Voice #1: tha's dad, man, you
know, shi' . . .

Anonymous Voice #2: ate a han'ful o' reds,
man . . .

Jack Webb: 10:28 a.m. Observed suspect leaving vicinity . . .

A.V. #1: don' dig tha' shi', man, an' i run . . .

J.W.: 10:53 a.m. Approached vehicle driven
by suspect.

New A.V.: [bellowing] Hey Ho'!

Orchestra . . . Dum, Da Dum Dum . . .

A.V. #2: tha's cooooooooold, hunhh, man . . .

Shrill, Piping Voice: Daddy, Daddy, Daddy! I
only have one cavity!!

New A.V.: Hey Ho'!

A.V. #1: kick yo' punk ass . . .

Unctuous Announcer: the whole idea behind
Crest . . .

This delightful audio montage is the invariable accompaniment of my literary endeavors.
If, therefore, these are sometimes a bit discon-
nected, or laced with the flavor of gall, I do
not apologize, but plead mitigating circumstances.

Karlene's Journal (cont'd.)

As we were leaving, the guard said, "they could use some new blood in here," just as Eugene was delayed in entering our exit cage. I thought I had seen a smile on his face—this guard was new to us—and I was hoping he was just being friendly. But other people thought he was saying, "We need some new *bloods* in here" and, of course, were angered. Ralph complained to Donnelly about it and they held a brief conference. The prison staff seems to hate the class; they resent students and hate "coddling" the inmates. But Donnelly, despite the obstacle of his staff's attitudes, needs to appease the liberal public who are now clamoring for reform at Soledad. So he's in a double bind. I think he *wants* to be humane; he was upset with Ralph's report of the guard's comment.

I suspect that change is inevitable. But the races must be able to adapt to these changes and without fear of being incarcerated for expressing their feelings. Time after time we read in the newspaper of some race being abused by the pigs. The ultimate thing is jail and prison. Why do most of the public have to take this kind of harassment?—in a society of liberty and justice! (What justice?) Being oneself is beautiful but can it be rewarding for the person who has a record behind him. I suggest not.

Theodore Martinez
B-24564 Soledad

Karlene's Journal (cont'd.)

The guard stopped me as I was leaving and asked me to identify the young "neegro" girl with "all the hair." I said there were two (thinking of Zena and Debra). After some fumbling, he said, "the one that is absent." Robbie? "That's it—Robbie Freeman." I followed him to the office in the rear of the building where the guard and the associate superintendent quietly conferred, both nodding their heads with tight-lipped tension. I asked them to explain the problem and they replied, "We've identified her—she's on the Soledad Defense Committee and she visits an inmate here charged with the murder of a guard—she can't play it both ways"—At this very moment Donnelly was telling Ralph that there had been an [FBI?] check on all of us and that Robbie can't return. This is dumbfounding—especially since several other members of the class have been working with the Committee and attending the hearings at Salinas. We gather in the parking lot . . . I wonder why there is always such a bitter, harsh wind blowing at Soledad? . . . and crowd into the van for a meeting before leaving the prison grounds. Realizing that if we protest Robbie's dismissal, the whole class is liable to cancellation, we decide to lie low, though with sharp ambivalence.

Arthur's Journal (cont'd.)

Wednesday, April 28, 1971 (Fifth Meeting)

Nothing very much happened—perhaps we were all too surprised and relieved that the class was meeting at all. Immediately prior to Politics 190c, the same room was the scene of a tense meeting (which I did not attend) between Asst. Super. Donnelly and members of the Inmate Advisory Council, the only officially sanctioned inmate organization for presenting grievances to the management. There was, two nights ago, a definitely non-sanctioned presentation of grievances to the management by inmates from "Whitney Hall"—there was a demonstration in short, which was terminated in a considerable amount of informal but skillful target practice on the windows of the school buildings.

The result was that Whitney Hall is on lock-up status and innumerable frantic meetings, frequently involving inmates, are being held, the one mentioned above being one. The result for our class: a future imperiled; four inmates missing and a fifth yanked out of class with record-breaking rudeness. Considering that the inmate so summoned is on excellent terms with the management, and was presumably being consulted in a capacity of responsible inmate voice, one may speculate on the vigor with which an inmate might be removed for disciplinary reasons.

That is more than enough of that depressing subject. Some time late in the a.m. session, the Santa Cruz representatives (I think Ben and Frank explained that a meeting the previous day at the university had produced the conclusion that the subject of utopias was in general too broad for the term papers (I will call them that to avoid confusion); that we would break the topic up into manageable pieces; each student would write on one or two of these topics and a similar subdivision would (more or less) guide the group discus-

The rules in this society are ideals written but then there are also unwritten rules like psychic violence which are understood. Once psychic violence is done away with, all other things that are so-called crimes will disappear. It is a cycle: once something is gone, the rest will follow.

Alma Cota
Crown UCSC

Karlene's Journal (cont'd.)

Wednesday, April 28, 1971 (Fifth Meeting)

Robbie is conspicuously absent today. As is Donald. The unofficial word is that he has been "transferred"—where? no one knows.

Ben reports on yesterday's meeting on campus of the UCSC members of the class: the dilemma of retaining the loose interaction of the Soledad class, yet not letting ideas continually fragment as they have so often; and above all dealing with the challenge of a gut search through our collective realities while seeking visions of utopian alternatives.

Ralph makes the proposal, readily accepted, that each student now select a single institutional topic for a final project. Not unexpectedly, most people choose topics centered around primarily either prison or school.

I express my frustration at the incongruity of dealing with literature and ideas that reflect white, middle-class consciousness and values, when we are largely a Third-World group. There is much positive response to the plea that we treat the material of the utopian genre as one which, from a minority-group perspective, needs to be continually criticized and analyzed and challenged—what applies and what does not? We further discuss the way in which at the last meeting we had divided spontaneously into three ethnically separate groups. Our common plea is that we get our heads together, here and now, if we are really serious when we talk equality and brotherhood, never mind political revolution.

I am moved at this point to tell the class about my experience with the Ras Tafarians—such a clear example of utopian socialism that I wonder why I haven't introduced it before now.

In mid-afternoon a very belligerent guard enters our midst at a time when the vibes are particularly good: heads together in a serious exchange of persons and ideas. The guard's

To me we speak of changing society. Assuming we are for *real*, we must totally dedicate ourselves for the need of change. We must not let threats of repression stop us from working with these goals. We must (those dedicated) "swim like fish in the ocean" to break down those barriers of the "oppressor."

Roberto Arras
B-24050 Soledad

Arthur's Journal (cont'd.)

sions. Two rather fascinating raps filled out
the remainder of the morning; Frank, with
occasional help from Mona, on the Mennon-
ites; and Karlene on turn-of-the-century California utopian communities, this evolving into
a discussion of the militant, articulate and
heavily persecuted Jamaican followers of H.
Selassie, whose movement names I cannot even
spell phonetically. From Karlene's charged
description, they are simply incredible, quite
aside from their erudition and enormous Afro
hairstyles; they apparently follow Savannarola
a bit as well as Emperor Selassie, judging from
their blood-and-brimstone Biblical outpourings,
backed up by fearsome drumming.

Afternoon

The afternoon opened with a rather weird,
but ultimately successful, effort at selecting
term paper topics. Karlene explained with
great clarity and small effect, that those who
had selected the topic for their paper should
write this topic down on a slip of paper; persons who had *not* chosen a topic were to
write two or three candidates on a slip of
paper unsigned, which would be used in some
random drawing process to assign topics that
appeared to be of considerable interest to the
class. There was certainly no difficulty in as-
certaining which topics were of general interest; but when these were written on slips of
paper, mixed, and presented to those students
who had not indicated any preference for
assignment through the luck of the draw, a
curious thing developed: it turned out that
everybody had a clear preference (or at least
some overwhelming aversions) after all. Thus
prodded, everybody (except Zena) quickly
signed up when the topics that had received
two or more nominations (i.e., appeared at
least twice among the slips of paper, signed

Karlene's Journal (cont'd.)

entrance is startling as he calls the name of
one of the inmates. Inmate X bolts and stands
upright. (Is that fear and humiliation on his
face?) "The captain wants to see you—*now*"—
Accusing, authoritarian—Get your jacket." I
hand X the history text I have brought for
him, (he wants to review the Constitution and
the Bill of Rights.) He tensely, nervously,
shame-facedly leaves; the guard follows close
behind him. We all fall into an embarrassed
silence which makes it difficult for us to continue. Is he really an informer as some in the
class have speculated? Whitney Hall is in lock-
up and several inmates are absent today (in
addition to Donald). X was seen in the Donnelly staff meeting which caused our class to
be held up. If not an informer could he be in
trouble? Could he be an organizer? A double
agent? Strange words. Paranoia engulfs us. *Do*
they listen to us through those omni-present
speakers in the ceiling? Probably. *Are* there
informers? We can only continue, for the sake
of the group's coherence and productivity as
though there are not.

As I exit from the lobby, coming from behind the students, the collection of guards
who stand outside our "classroom" are commenting on the "pretty long hair" of some of
the male students—"Hey, Tiny Tim! Did you
see that guy?"

Arthur's Journal (cont'd.)

and unsigned, that were turned in) were put
on the board. What would Frazier think of
this inadvertent bit of behavioral engineering,
I wonder? Anyway, the topics, with the number of nominations each received, are listed
below (Karlene and I have separate lists of
who is writing on each one and there is no
need to repeat that information here).

Education (12), Penal Systems (11), Courts
and Police (5), Family (2), Religion and
Church (2), Welfare (2), Military (2), Politics
and Government and Revolution (3), Psychological Preparation for Utopia (1).

These topics except for the last one, to
which I am irrevocably committed by four
pages of my convoluted prose, reflect the decision to focus the class attention on some of
the more practical aspects of utopian planning,
to wit: the past failings and desirable future
configurations of common social institutions.
Of course, we as a class really had no choice.
We are not, individually, Huxleys or even
Skinners, and creative semi-fiction cannot be
performed as a team effort. The net talent
brought to bear on the problem would NOT
equal the sum of the individual participating
talents (indeed it might well be smaller than
the least of them). . . So the subdivision into
bite-sized topics really had to be done. If we
do not end up with a model utopian society,
we at least should have some of the theoretical
building blocks, which is a good deal better
than nothing.

We are so desperately short of class time
(perhaps here is the place to mention, for
whatever guidance it may provide, that the
time is precious to the inmates to a degree
that is singularly poignant)—why was I almost
apologetic in my suggestion that we consider
skipping the long noon break, thereby adding
a useable 33% to the class time? The vote, con-

On a continuum between the totally intolerable society and the completely fantastic things as they might be, our class must occupy a tense picket line on the way to fantastic. Met by the specific wish of each of us, we are still quite unfree under the circumstances. We listen respectfully (no mean accomplishment): though we may not always succeed in saying the important things, we manage it from time to time. The time in session goes so quickly and our sense of cohesiveness is constantly being destroyed by the clock. There is no dull moment; if we find it difficult to pursue a topic to conclusion it is usually because so many other worthy topics present themselves in mid-course. I admit to having held some other hopes. I had indeed hoped a general utopia could be outlined among us. Not so much for the product as for the process. If it is true, as has been expressed, that there are basic things we agree on, it should be possible to discover and define them, and comforting in view of our diversity to uncover a community of shared beliefs.

Mona Burns
College V UCSC

Arthur's Journal (cont'd.)

fined to the inmates was as I recall instantaneous and unanimous in favor of spending the lunch period in class. And the lunches here really are not that bad. The display of affirmative hands snapping upward should have been very rewarding to Dr. Guzman and his faithful staff and students, who leave a very nice place to make a long drive to a place which is not nice at all. I fervently hope the wind-up men who control such things will not conclude that our desire for an unbroken class day conceals some sinister purpose, and that, if the plan is implemented, it is not too hard on the digestions of the Santa Cruz contingent. I have myself always suffered from a far more voracious intellectual than gastronomic appetite, but I cannot be sure this peculiarity is universally shared.

Wednesday, May 5, 1971 (Sixth Meeting)

God DAMN the noxious voice of the tee vee; four hours per day (six on Saturday and Sunday) without reprieve it bores into my cell and skull. I stuff newspaper around my door, and wet toilet paper plugs into my ears, and all the good it does is to give me "Gunsmoke" at 60 db instead of the 120 ambient outside. Two weeks of producing reasoned prose in the midst of this electronic bedlam is getting to me. I am going to produce some unreasoned prose. Class today was a bust and I am tired of doing book reviews. Screw the assignment. Make me Flunkie for the day; give me an "F" in place of a color-coordinated washer/dryer/bidet and an evil-smelling kiss from Jack Bailey. My GPA is suffering from over confidence.

The p.m. subgroup I was in accomplished nothing at all toward advancing the progress of the course, and a good deal toward providing the inmate participants with a rare, desperately needed commodity: unstructured

After four weeks I am completely satisfied with our progress. The class has awakened many areas to me as an individual—shown me ways of life I was never hep to before. Switched on many lights in my mind.

William Lute
B-25871-B Soledad

There is a front stage and back stage Amerika, and too often it is hard to tell who is hidden and who is visible. Backstage lies a plethora of smoldering talent and power within the ranks of iconoclastic youth, revolutionary blacks, progressive liberals, and resurrected conservatives. Rather than emigration to the suburbs, and exodus to the communes, rather than burn it down—we should all come together with this common objective to make it better. But of course this involves genuine effort, and real dedication to the principle of human rights for everyone; and any concept of a utopian society should be for the benefit of *all the people.* That is to say, the development of utopia will start with the redevelopment of the society as it now exists.

Richard Risher
B-21915 Soledad

I have gotten a great deal from the class—I can now express myself and my feelings toward people who I know will listen.

Theodore Martinez
B-24564 Soledad

Arthur's Journal (cont'd.)

conversation and rapport with free human beings. You can get very tired of an unvaried social diet of scaggy studs in faded canvas clothes, even the more elegant ones who have learned tricks besides spitting and twirling their keychains. I have an odd notion that the peculiar problems of conducting a class of mixed free and imprisoned students may require a radical departure from the usual classroom scenario. Possibility: structure the first half rigidly (anything less than fairly rigid adherence to a topic invariably drifts into pleasant random chatter); get the lecture, if any, the assignments, announcements, and other business over with; read a few outstanding written contributions, and then succumb to conversational anarchy. It's bound to happen anyway to one degree or another. I mean acknowledged anarchy: no assigned topic, not even a hint that the subject matter should have any connection with the class. The only rule should be that the scowling faces peering in through the observation ports should perceive an appropriate decorum. Make up for it by cracking the whip on the written part of the class effort, if it appears that the class progress is really impeded to a significant degree.

The Alternative requires some kind of comment. I'll begin with the title: it should be *an Alternative*. (I don't mean this literally, but the book focuses on the rural commune, which is only one of a number of approaches to an alternative life style.) It's beautiful and it won't work for very long, nor on a very large scale. The communes described by Hedgepeth are the models for an absolutely self-destroying society; the harsh facts of economics suggest the reason. The communes are (usually out front and invariably in fact) existing on the unmissed surplus of an enormously wealthy nation. Food stamps, donations, letters from home, windfall capitalization, the side of crafts: all impossible except in a country so

Now if the people involved with the writing of the book [*The Alternative*] were sincere in their effort to paint a clear picture of what the actual reasons behind the so-called hippie movement were about, they have done a good job ... If communal living is the answer, which does seem logical, I still can't understand how they hope to convert the masses with this idea.

Ruben Gonzales
B-28988 Soledad

Arthur's Journal (cont'd.)

glutted with material wealth that it cheerfully finances its radicals, subversives, dropouts, and non-productive visionaries. If a significant fraction of the population took to leather-craft and scratch-plowing in the best tradition of the sixteenth century, the unmissed surplus would rapidly turn into a clearly perceived deficit, and we would return posthaste to that unlamented state where almost everybody busted his ass eighteen hours a day just to keep his belly full. The youth communes of Hedgepeth's essay are essentially retreats, wherein a small fraction of the general population (at any one time) can escape the horrors of a depersonalized and mechanized society. Viewed in this light, they are viable; they may be the saving of a generation; and I will even buy the thesis that everybody should spend some fraction of his existence in one. But retreats, whether religious, primitive-agricultural, or academic, can at best be temporary places of refuge for those in special need, if for no other reason than that they are exceedingly inefficient collective endeavors (like the Soviet farms) they cease utterly to serve their original purpose. Let me state that I am in complete sympathy with most of the aims and policies of the rural communes. Their benign anarchy, their tolerance of eccentricity, their animals, and the earth they work—these are noble concepts. Perhaps someone will eventually figure out a way to merge them into an economically practical framework. That would be a giant step toward utopia.

I feel running, talking, and praying won't cure the ills of the U.S.A. Some type of action is needed related to love of your fellow man after you've destroyed the choking roots of the ruling class. I'm sorry that I can't elaborate more on this book [*The Alternative*] but it doesn't give me the drive or purpose I'm seeking.

Phillip Jacobs
B-21434-A Soledad

The theme of almost all the communes depicted centered about a return to a past or golden age. Again and again, the theme of back to the soil, manual labor, and simple old time religion, is repeated with variations on the theme. The christian concepts in calvinism, romanism, and fundamentalism helped to create the monster society from which so many communes wish to escape. The hard-work ethic, the repression of sexual needs, and visionary elitism (chosen people) all evolved from Judaic-Christian theology. The communes by retaining some christian practices are in a sense planting the seeds of their own destruction.

Ben Dunn
Merrill UCSC

The togetherness, the sharing, mutual respect is what life is all about. Being capable of loving: the people are so beautiful in *Alternative*, it seems to make me feel so ugly or super ignorant!

William Lute
B-25871-B Soledad

The search for alternatives (to the existing system) is valid. However, a mass self-withdrawal into intentional communes (utopias) is not in my opinion the way to change this society into an *ideal* society. In our search for alternatives to the bullshit that society wants to force-feed us, we must develop a fidelity and consistency within ourselves first. If it is inconsistent for a nation to go to the moon while

Arthur's Journal (cont'd.)

Once, back in the days before God invented technicolor, and the world was perceived clearly in black and white, I managed to inveigle an eminently respectable college out of a M.S. (in physics) without writing a thesis at all. I am thus prepared to look with some awe at anyone who has managed to produce a thesis, particularly as an undergraduate. But I think even if I were not so predisposed I some of its citizens are starving then it is no less inconsistent for us not to get involved in changing things merely because of some hang-ups we might have about being co-opted by the establishment. The commune represents in many ways a cop-out. What happens is people who become fed-up with things (socially) symbolically throw in the towel, and split to the unrealistic and false security of the intentional commune. In effect, this is the same move made by middle-Amerika in their panic-striken flight to suburbia. No one becomes concerned with changing things for the better (an attempt toward a real utopia, meaning to include all people) just making things more comfortable for the individual. In our search for utopia we must be wary of the human failings of selfishness, despair, and frustration. If we are serious about being fed-up with the way things are going in this society, and are sincerely interested with making it better (utopia?) then we must efficiently and systematically tackle the problems of anomie, alienation, riots, war, genocide, pollution, congestion, degenerative and mental disease, and so on. To become involved and concerned on this level we will find ourselves paying particular attention to persons and neighborhoods, which is very different from the withdrawal approach. We will need all available human resources in a consecrated effort to change this society for the better. Call it utopia, ideal or whatever— the movement is for the improvement of the society in which we find ourselves today.

Richard Risher
B-21915 Soledad

Karlene's Journal (cont.

Wednesday, May 5, 1971 (Sixth Meeting)

Today's discussion of *Walden II* is initially dominated by Francisco; his intellectual energy catalyzes a good discussion.

Leaving at noon to return to a Santa Cruz commitment, I find myself deluged with questions. The men need things—books we've promised to bring, papers to submit or criticisms to read from earlier writings, questions about writing problems, personal interests that need pursuing but can't be dealt with in the whole

Arthur's Journal (cont'd.)

would find "One Love—One Heart—One Destiny" [An undergraduate thesis written by Karlene Faith] a remarkable paper. I certainly do not feel any inhibitions about commenting on it simply because my comments are to be submitted, in the way of a normal class assignment, to its author. Its exotic subject matter alone would set Karlene's paper apart. Added to that is the bizarre picture, purely imaginary I would suspect, of Mrs. F. finishing up a round of housewifely duties—getting the children off to school and the like—and scuttling off into the bush to share a revolutionary discourse and a dollop of hasheesh with her incredible companions. And companions, rather than subjects, they clearly were. Mrs. Faith's sympathy for, and identification with, the Ras Tafarians shines from every page of the thesis, giving it the liveliness not often discernible in academic papers.

Wednesday, May 17, 1971 (Seventh Meeting)

The New Conservatives

Today was conservative's day in Politics 190c. That is to say, the third world (racist swine that I am, I failed to capitalize "third" on the first try; let us have it again), no, Third World members of the class gave a lengthy, relatively clear, and intensely interesting exposition of their particular view of a number of topics related to the utopian idea, most notably communes rural and urban, drugs and drug sellers, and students-as-tenants. Their view was of such great interest to me because it reflected, with uncanny accuracy many of the cherished notions of the extreme right (hence the opening sentence of this diatribe). We are all familiar with the reverse racism popular with the more militant Black (note the cap. B—on the first try) organizations—

Now getting back to traditional dog-eat-dog-ism in America, American cutthroatism, the estrangement, and exploitation, oppression, war capitalism, wage slavery, mis-education, imperialism, individualism, power elite-ism and hope-to-die-police-state-ism-by-1973-or-bust. Yes, come on with the alternative! Although the communes and other socialist cooperatives are embryonic at this stage, they are saying a whole lot in terms of humanist principles and the humanization of human life. The application of scientific innovation is not yet the common denominator for all communes but the more progressive communes are usually the most scientific.

Sherwin Forté
B-21899 Soledad

I firmly believe that Third-World people would totally dismiss the idea of a big brother. We tend to be skeptical, and not easily swayed by Hitler-like tactics.

Plezena Shack
Merrill UCSC

We are as racially segregated mid-course as on the first day, though there hasn't been a single instance of any kind of animosity directed towards a person.

Mona Burns
College V UCSC

And although we are different in color, can we not as human beings put our heads together to form what we consider to be "a true meaning of life?" My guess is no . . . I consider the revolution the most constructive alternative. For the reason that it deals with downright facts about what this society is and what the ultimate thing can be.

Theodore Martinez
B-24564 Soledad

Karlene's Journal (cont'd.)

group—such a chaotic departure. Ralph is justifiably bothered by the confusion and the continued inability of all of us to abruptly say good-bye at the moment the guard enters to release us—that goddam hostile guard, noisily, antagonizingly jangling his keys. What an uptight class this has been today—for so many reasons which I'm too weary even to comment upon. We simply must next time relax together.

Wednesday, May 12, 1971 (Seventh Meeting)

In discussing the *Alternative* most of us concur with Phillip's angry observation that to enter a rural commune is a luxury that only the white middle class can afford. At the same time many of us are unwilling to negate the potential significance and value of them. I suggest that communes, for example, may provide a rest-home function for frustrated alternative-seeking youth who may later return to the larger society with renewed perspective and energies and clearer priorities. Ralph takes issue with the implication that whites have some special need to escape to a peace-giving solitude. He reminds us that everyone, and especially struggling minority peoples, could use and should be entitled to that kind of retreat and privilege. It is suggested that the public often supports communes at least to the extent that it ignores them because it effectively removes potential troublemakers from the mainstream of society. And yet communitarians feel they are effecting change if only by example. To this extent, communes attack cultural systems while copping out on political issues.

Courtney: The Haight failed because of drugs and the ghetto atmosphere. It pushed the Blacks out to make room for rich kids who were escaping from suburbia to romanticize

Arthur's Journal (cont'd.)

US, the Black Muslims, the BPP—it is presumably the Anglo conscience that makes reverse racism socially acceptable. Anyone who doubts that Black racism is tolerable where white would be greeted with howls of outrage may consider the media: "Black is Beautiful". . . "Soul Everything". . ."Black Power": these are so chic they are beginning to be used as advertising slogans. It is difficult to imagine the fuss that would ensue if someone started shouting "Aryan Power" or "White is Right" over the tube, even for so innocent a purpose as the marketing of Swedish crystal. What delighted me in class was a discussion of white students and/or hippies moving into a Black ghetto neighborhood. From the tone of the discussion I would not have been surprised to hear somebody remark seriously that "white hippies (or students) are ok, but I wouldn't want one to move in next door to me." There was also an amazing bit of dialog condemning students for raising rents in poor neighborhoods (where someone thoughtlessly located a university) by dint of eleven of them cramming into a two-bedroom apartment, whose exhorbitant rent split 11 ways was in accord with the student purse. No slumlord ever concocted a more devilish rationalization.

There was some interesting exposition by Courtney on the response of the Black residents of the Haight-Ashbury of the invasion of young, Anglo wanderers a few years ago. Courtney identified the Haight as "part of the Fillmore District" (the Fillmore District is a distinctly Black area in San Francisco). I am not an expert on the demography of the city but I am reasonably sure that the Haight was never a part of the Fillmore District; rather it was a distinct slum, mixed racially rather than predominately Black, and separate and identifiable to the same degree as Chinatown, the Tenderloin, North Beach, Hunter's Point, and the other unofficial districts of San

Also equally doubtful is harmony between blacks and whites though it is possible if a little understanding is applied. Frankly, I can foresee a building of the youths of this country in harmony against the sick society struggle and so forth. And harmony later on, but at the moment, I'll base my views mainly on the Third World movement . . . the day when whites, blacks, brown and yellow can put aside the color issue to unite and build a world where men can be understanding and passionate—then and only then will the destructive might of the military not be needed.

Phillip Jacobs
B-21434-A Soledad

Karlene's Journal (cont'd.)

the slums; the peace signs were substituted by guns when the police moved in.

Francisco: Communal living can be counter-revolutionary—it's happening in Santa Cruz. Students as a collective group can afford to pay $250 a month for a very modest house, so that the rents go up and there is no low-cost housing available for the poor.

Ruben Reyna: I can respect the human values of communes but I can't respect people turning their backs on social problems . . . going off to the woods to practice brotherhood while their brothers are fighting and dying in the streets.

Richard: And yet we can't deny the value of communes.

Ralph: When I see kids swarm to the subsistence life of which in my youth I was ashamed, I am encouraged. It raises my estimation of my own early life.

But I recall Zena's disgust toward a visiting professor's "hippie" garb—"we were always poor but we were always clean and well-dressed; to dress like that is like poking fun at the poor." Phillip and Courtney are frustrated by the amount of time that is spent sitting around talking about the problems when people should be busy eliminating them.

Richard: But before we can eliminate a problem we have to educate people to the nature of the problem.

Eugene: It is through shared resistance, action and repression that radicalization begins. And the hippies are beginning to be repressed.

Arthur's Journal (cont'd.)

Francisco. In any case the Black residents seemed to view the hippies as invading colonists who were bent on the same sinister mission as the corrupt urban planner who wishes to eradicate substandard housing and build in its place high-rise condominiums—on land owned by his cousin: the elimination of the Black indigenous residents. In point of fact the early hippies settled in the Haight for almost the same reason anyone else might— low rents combined with a tolerance for such eccentricities as zoning violations and late-night racket. A little later the community aspect—the reputation of the Haight as the scene of the action—of course attracted a large number of wandering young persons. Courtney pointed out that the hippies would not adapt to the life style of the Black ghetto and did not establish much rapport with their Black neighbors, even fearing that they (the hippies) might be victims of assaults and robberies perpetrated by said neighbors, a prophecy which Courtney said turned out to be self-fulfilling. The implication that the hippies, by failing to adopt an utterly alien life-style solely because it was the habit of the neighborhood, qualified themselves as fair game for criminal activity, is very clear. It is remarkable that the red-necked inhabitants or rural villages use exactly the same logic in justifying their persecution of any long hairs that happen to take up residence in their vicinity; another example, I suggest, of the basically right-wing flavor of much of the vaunted Black consciousness.

Karlene's Journal (cont'd.)

Ralph: When I observed white, middle class kids getting beaten and rounded up by the police at protest riots I say 'welcome to the status of a minority group.'

Deirdre: But going to jail is becoming a fad; they aren't learning anything by their busts.

Francisco: There's no special badge for the poor who go to jail. I'm not going to throw rocks and get hit on the head. I figure I've already paid my dues. Some white kid can say, "We know how you feel, brother." Well, fuck you, brother.

Courtney: Why don't we do away with the police. They don't protect us anyway. Let's all in our own communities protect ourselves.

Richard: All the riots and looting that follows—blacks looting blacks . . . points out the necessity of educating our own people about what the problems really are . . . we can't be stealing from each other.

Ralph: So how do we raise the level of awareness?

Many voices respond to the command that we've got to get the goods from the man—take back all of that which our labor has provided them.

Ralph: O.K., you and I are privy to information as to the source of the problems. But now what? I think that Richard's point raises a very fundamental question.

Ruben Reyna: [agreeing with Ralph] Don't put your politics into my life. I don't want that dollar or that Cadillac. I can live on the earth, and that's all I want.

I know the government is trying to stop them from doing what they want because they [the hippies] are his children so they cannot make it even if they want to.

Courtney Cain
B-26494 Soledad

Arthur's Journal (cont'd.)

Diligent probing reveals that marijuana may be a special case not requiring the degree of proscription accorded to the opiates. The Black view, as expressed by the class, appears to lump everything else with smack. Although the descriptive terminology ("shoot" . . . "strung out" . . . "paper" . . . "nodding out" . . .) relates directly to heroin, somewhat to the most desperate extremes of amphetamine and/or barbiturate involvement, it never relates to the psychedelics. "Hard drugs like LSD and heroin . . . " is a phrase that

Karlene's Journal (cont'd.)

Courtney: But man they'll get you there. They'll tax you—they'll divide it up—and you won't have that land.

In the afternoon, our small group *now a complete racial mix*, discussed drugs. Exchanges become increasingly and intensely personal. Bill defended the use of drugs as personal choice, insisting that if social and psychological conditions were stable, heroin addiction would not be a social problem. There was general disagreement to Bill's defense of heroin, though the feeling was shared that the public attack on drugs was to cut off the tail of the dragon while leaving the monster intact. The atmosphere is reassuringly open and filled with a sense of emerging trust.

Arthur's Journal (cont'd.)

could only come from a police department flyer or a black militant speech—another point in my case to the effect that, whatever the current tactical antagonism may be, the two groups share a sizeable chunk of common philosophy. Whatever the ravages of heroin may be in the ghetto and the *barrio*, in an overall sense the ravages of alcohol are certainly far worse (I am not saying that booze is worse than smack from the standpoint of the individual user; I am merely stating that the total social cost of the grape exceeds that of the poppy, because of vastly more widespread distribution). Now the ghettos and *barrios* are awash in liquor stores, bars, taverns, without these worthy commercial enterprises having attracted the lethal attention of the BPP—indeed the Demon Rum is worshipped assiduously by those who can least afford the price of tribute. This is remarkably reminiscent of the attitude of the typical Wallacite, who noisily favors hanging marijuana smokers—particularly after he has oiled his tonsils with a half case of Coors. A minor point, perhaps, but it further supports my current thesis that we have in our midst a strange new brand of conservatism.

Wednesday, May 19, 1971 (Eighth Meeting)

I couldn't attend the morning sessions as the result of a communication breakdown. I should not have made the mistake of conferring with a staff member within minutes of the news of violence at Central; but I was personally unaware of this incident and wandered into a *faux pas* that could have had disastrous consequences. Fortunately, some of the noble souls on the staff who keep their cool (like Rich Hughes) managed to straighten everything out. It is such things that contribute to the unreality, the Kafka-haunted paranoia of prison.

All this led to a potpourri of search which began with the social phenomena which occurred in the Haight-Ashbury district of San Francisco ... all they have to do is cut their hair and put on a pair of "A-1" slacks and become part of society again ... this privilege the blacks and *chicanos* do not have.

Joaquin Castro
Cowell College

If you've had it, touched it, it is easier to reject it, because you already know what it is like. It's not easy to reject it, even though you want to reject it, if you've never had it.

Alma Cota
Crown UCSC

I could not help but think of the migrant farmworkers who could little afford to stash funds for the winter and who simply and "naturally" starved when farmwork was scarce. Their rough life was not by choice. Therein lies the reason for my impatience in trying to relate to white groups who seem to think that self-denial of lavish, material things will purge them of their "crime" of being comfortable WASPS.

Rebeca Alicia Lopez
Merrill UCSC

Karlene's Journal (cont'd.)

Wednesday, May 19, 1971 (Eighth Meeting)

The days at Soledad are consistently tension laden but none so severely as this. We are told upon entering North that our meeting place has been changed. The students wait in the lounge while I go to Donnelly's office to make enquiry—as I stand alone there waiting to see him, someone rushes in and exclaims that a guard has just been knifed by two inmates. I leave immediately and go to the cafeteria to tell Ralph what I have just heard. After a long delay, we are admitted to a staff meeting room where the class is to be held. The day is fraught with conflict and anxiety for everyone involved.

On the way home, I ask Gary Pernell if he would record the day's events—I didn't feel I could do it. The following are his notes:

We were prepared before class not to expect anything in the way of involvement, etc., from the inmates. We were also informed that there were "weird vibes" today. The class was ready to begin when we were escorted into a

Arthur's Journal (cont'd.)

My thanks to Karlene for halting discussion of the *Sane Society* when such a discussion was palpably impossible in the prevailing atmosphere. It is a measure of the insanity that clings to all of us that this step—eminently reasonable, in fact the only possible rational course under the circumstances—seemed somehow very daring. We talk of utopia, of revolutionary change, of liberation, and then we are afraid to pee until the bell rings, and we sit in straight rows just as we were taught to do by some dessicated spinster when we were in grammar school. Congratulations for a practical demonstration of sensitive and relative education; small though the incident might have been, it was action instead of intent and endless tape-loop dialog.

Regarding Dr. Guzman's reiterated intention to publish something assembled (at least in part) from the class writings, a clear distinction must be made between a paper *about* the class and one incorporating the class's written contributions; or some of them. The former, particularly if it contains a lot of statistics about number of essays written, attendance records, relative performance of students and inmates, etc., may be an academic and aesthetic horror, and meaningless besides, but could be a persuasive argument in the effort to continue a program of classes like Politics 190c inside the prison system. The things written by class members, free and imprisoned alike, would probably not be pleasing to those whose favor will be needed if Soledad is to have a continuing program of college-level courses. Quite aside from my own polemics which discretion might cause to be delicately set aside for future publication—say in about 2047—there is quite a lot of anti-establishment bias apparent in the class. Yet it is to aft starboard pillars of the establishment that appeal must be made if classes are to continue. I hope this problem will be considered

. . . As soon as you find a teacher who is trying to help you, it's time to leave—to go to another town where the teacher doesn't care about you. You end up the rest of the year learning nothing and getting angry at the situation and frustrated because you are not learning anything. You stand next to a building watching the other children play. You don't know anybody. Teachers label you as "latecomers" and separate you from the others. Schools try to find out about your family. You don't want to talk about it, if it's going to be used against you in an embarrassing way, so you are ashamed to tell them your background. Kids tell you you talk funny because you talk with an accent. Wherever you were born, in the United States or Mexico, you are still considered a foreigner.

Alma Cota
Crown UCSC

new fishbowl (complete with full-view windows). Minutes later the inmates entered. Were we supposed to feel fortunate that only five were missing?

The discussion began and the real (immediate) problems of the prison were ignored. The full story of the murder of justifiable homicide (if "they" can use the term so can "we") of a program administrator at Central came out later. He was killed by two white inmates which seemed to indicate that things had really been building up; since racism is used every day against Third-World inmates, conditions must have been totally unbearable for all.

Ralph introduced our guest, the Provost of a new college at UCSC, a utopian experiment which we perhaps could relate to. He was immediately challenged as to how he could accept traditionally defined roles in a bureaucracy and attempt to de-bureaucratize them. He let us know he was always open to new ideas and is willing to re-evaluate his progress at any time. Many of us, especially inmates, thought him rather naive about Third-World problems. Many of us were curious to hear how he dealt with his authority position when it came to decision making. He could only tell us that he was attempting to be sensitive to the people he was working with and not override consensus decisions even when they opposed him. The question of Third-World support was posed. He explained that two or three Third-World students had been working with him in designing the college but the general response was slight. He also stated that 14 of the 20 faculty slots for next year have been filled by 3 women and 11 men . . . All white. He went on to inform us that it wasn't his fault since the boards of studies had been involved in most of the actual hiring.

After lunch all but one of the inmates (the

I hope someone will read my writing and prevent the chaos this nation is headed for. My feeling for the poor whites is comparable to a fellow soldier fighting the same battle, only in different units. In my blackness, I also recognize those of the middle class who are fighting to reform our sick society. For those people only do I have any compassion. The use of the political leaders' manipulation of the military as a sledge hammer of capitalism and its many evils is outrageous and should cease. Only by the masses' writing and battling those in power will a change be brought about.

Phillip Jacobs
B-21434-A Soledad

Arthur's Journal (cont'd.)

in the light of a suitable blend of resolution
and diplomacy.

" . . . The movement for change is
neither motivated by a desire to secure
privileges which have no relevance to
liberty, nor law having no force of
protective effect: the movement is a
spirit of youth weary with a society
permeated with a million varieties of
legal corruption, exploitation, systematic privation, wholesale slaughter both
domestic and abroad, perpetuation of
racism, hunger and crime. A spirit
which will not be intimidated by force,
bought off by temporary solutionism
of privilege or smothered by all the
law 'n order abbracadabra uttered by a
million vested interest law givers. We
will have positivity; the gods themselves know that today's static nega-
tively will be without anything to
stand and/or feed on tomorrow.
Nothing on earth or in heaven can
save the old order but a new beginning. We have already lost everything
but the right to be bullied, intimidated

Karlene's Journal (cont'd.)

local snitch?) was with us. Alma was asked to read her paper dealing with the many aspects of education which a migrant worker must go through. She detailed the lack of stability and understanding that farmworkers are given in schools. This was related to the family structure and economic conditions which force a child to attend 10 to 15 different schools. When Alma finished Sherwin acknowledged that while he was not raised under those conditions, he could relate to many of the situations which Alma described. Then Joaquin asked the visiting provost if he could understand, and told him that this was more than just a piece of writing. The response was intense to Alma's paper—and affirmative—it reminded members of the class of the personal bases for their anger against the system.

I'm not sure of the order in which the following happened but they should be noted: Karlene read a paper which Deirdre had written on freedom and liberty, which ended with a quote from a brother at Folsom. A silent respect followed the reading and later many of the inmates who had not previously talked with Deirdre sought her out and expressed their interest and admiration to her as the result of her paper. Earlier Karlene had asked why the previous week's meeting had been so good. Randomly noted, the responses were— *Alternative* was a good basis for a critical discussion; the subject was carried at a very personal level. Time is running short and there is much to be said and done.

Arthur's Journal (cont'd.)

Regarding Dr. Guzman's forthcoming speech before a collection of Los Angeles law enforcement officers: Dr. Guzman has very likely never experienced anything like the mental state of a law enforcement officer. I have. As a hired technical prostitute to several Department of Defense contractors, it has been my privilege to work with, socialize with, and share the twisted philosophy of men dedicated to enforcing their national customs and beliefs on an unwilling world, using the simplest and least effective of all teaching tools: naked, murderous force. I have enthused over the latest techniques for killing Russians or Chinese by tens of millions, and participated in hideously smug discussions proving that this barbaric planning is perfectly justified for the defense of a vaguely threatened "American Way of Life." The L.A.P.D. are protecting the American Way of Life, Southern California Decadent Subdivision, from the threat posed by hippies, niggers and perverts. The police view themselves as the domestic and local arm of the military machine by which the earth is to be purged of all opposition to traditional American values and practices. Did you read that? Read it again. The palaver about "protect and serve" about "fighting crime" means exactly nothing except the extermination of all forms and signs of deviance from the accepted middle-class norms. The Blacks are not the only ones who have become politicized; the police have, too. A review of the public pronouncements of three L.A. police chiefs (Parker, Reddin, Davis) will show a clear emergence of neo-Fascist doctrine having exactly zero relevance to traditional concepts of police activity. The Los Angeles Police Dept. is a Political Police Force in the hallowed tradition of the NKVD and the Gestapo; its members are subject to political

and live as free souls . . . what could we possibly gain by half-stepping? A right to die deprived and miserable? No, sister, we who are spiritually obsessed have to fear only the becoming of abject cowards willing to live at the price of being morally, socially, and spiritually dead. Only two types of people fear censorship: cowards and those to whom truth is a complete stranger; neither of which can stand the sight of freedom. Freedom is not something which can be given to any of us . . . but an action *we must take* to know that it exists. The right to do something does not exist for that individual who never attempts its possesssion. And no amount of oppressive censorship can conceal a system so thoroughly corrupt, that to pass without the most rigorous condemnation it must pass unseen. Who can hide from the vast horror? Let them have their censorship and us our courage and we will win. Where the human intellect is inventive and courageous, all which comes under its penetrating scrutiny takes place in a glass house. Let us be right on . . . "

A Brother in Folsom Prison

Karlene's Journal (cont'd.)

The discussion for the day ended with Ralph revealing that he had been invited to speak before the Los Angeles Police Department. He asked the help of inmates in determining what material to include in his speech. Recommendations to the police via Ralph included being empathetic, hiring more Third-World cops, hiring more plain-clothes cops so the uniforms would not be so offensive. Many of these suggestions did not come from the inmates. Uniform treatment seemed to be the major request. Several members of the class wondered if this speech would have any good effect at all.

This disrespect of man's freedom of expression can be reviewed by the manner in which young men and women have been gunned down in the street. Kent State, Watts, Chicago. Another display of this madness was the brutal use of force just a few weeks ago in Washington. A strong national armed tactical force seems necessary, but only in *defense* of the poor against the mad ones in power, who are the main cause of discontent.

Phillip Jacobs
B-21434-A Soledad

Arthur's Journal (cont'd.)

indoctrination and are further pre-selected (often by a deliberate recruitment policy) from among persons of extreme rightward political bias; and its political uniformity is maintained by the fact that no one of moderate or liberal persuasion would remain for more than a brief time in its ranks.

It would be extremely naive to consider a gathering of LA policemen as an ordinary group of persons whose peculiar job has brought them into conflict with certain of the area's citizens, but who, on the whole, are reasonable men amenable to rational discourse. Nothing could be further from the truth. They are an elite, fanatical volunteer corps of warriors, in their own assessment carrying out a holy war against the forces of Satan. Their guns and clubs are the annointed swift swords of an avenging God, and nothing will deter them from their mission of sacred slaughter—certainly not one *Chicano* professor, probably a friend of that Goddamned Ruben Salazar who won't write no more lousy columns about police and malpractices, and probably also paid by the communists or the Jews to stir up trouble. I wish Dr. Guzman well, but I know too much about the sort of thinking, if it may be dignified by such a term, he will face, to expect that his address will accomplish much.

Random Comments on
The Sane Society

Time does not allow any sort of indepth discussion of Dr. Fromm's work; rather, I will spew out comments more or less at random, touching on the aspects of the book that seem to me most singular or memorable.

Dr. Fromm writing in the early fifties—the heyday of the Silent Generation, of which I am an anomalously unquiet member—antici-

Karlene's Journal (cont'd.)

Wednesday, June 2, 1971 (Final Meeting)

There is a terrible urgency felt throughout this meeting—so many practical tasks to take care of; collection and return of borrowed books; turning in of papers; answering of countless individual questions; exchanging addresses; etc.; and the terrible—mixed with some relief—acknowledgment that as a group we will never be together again. I ask each person in the class to write an autobiographical statement to be included in the book about this class (if we ever get it together) and ask that if anyone wishes his or her statement or any other writing published anonymously, they should indicate that (confidentially, to avoid peer pressure). A lot of the writings have been harsh indictments of the systems and could have repercussions for the inmates if their names are used. It is a testament to their courage that not one chose to remain anonymous. They have spoken from deep conviction and are willing to take responsibility for their words.

People respond to one another today with more than usual consideration. We are again meeting in the fishbowl and occasionally falter with inhibitions related to the vulnerability of our location, but a remarkable frankness occurred nonetheless. Delores Ramirez, who had participated in last year's class at Soledad, has returned for a visit, and although she is new to almost everyone, she eases comfortably into the discussion. She talks about her experience working in Mexico—teaching in an Indian village. The people's struggle to develop a political consciousness and their

Arthur's Journal (cont'd.)

pated many of the criticisms of current American society that have become hallmarks of the counter-culture. His analysis of alienation, of the estrangement of man from himself and from his fellows as well as from his planet, indicates he saw clearly in 1954, the evils that twenty years of agony have at last revealed to less perceptive analysts.

Dr. Fromm's suggested approach to remodeling society along viable lines are also prophetic, anticipating as they do many of the philosophical foundations of the communitarian movement of the sixties. Why in view of this, is Fromm not widely hailed as one of the prophets of the alternative society? Why does he not occupy a place with Herman Hesse, with Timothy Leary, even with Abbie Hoffman? I suggest it is because of what I am going to call the Psychologist's Syndrome (a more exact term would be the Psychologist-Turned-Writer-Syndrome) which Fromm shares with, among others, B. F. Skinner. It manifests itself in an uncanny ability to make the most exquisitely meritorious propositions appear unattractive. In the name of humanity, or humanism, those afflicted with Psychologist's Syndrome squeeze the last scintilla of humanity out of their theories; they deodorize and sterilize everything they touch until their product perishes out of sheer goodness. Like *Walden Two,* the Communities of Work that Dr. Fromm offers as prototype mini-societies are dull, *dull, DULL,* and clean, *clean, CLEAN,* to the point of suffocation. A radical child of the sixties trapped in such an environment would feel his palm itching for the feel of a Molotov cocktail in direct proportion to the stifling perfection of the world around him. I wonder if it is not a general failing of psychologist-philosophers that, in searching for a rational explanation for human behavior, they overlook the salient part of human nature that by definition will forever defy rational analysis

Karlene's Journal (cont'd.)

handicaps in achieving it. The people who come to teach are from the cities. "Cultured people" who have come to teach the "uncultured." Disappointment in elections. They put up candidates who win, but the government doesn't recognize them. Delores invests her hopes in educational possibilities. She's a good visitor—she has immediate rapport with the men.

Michael: This course has given us the realization that we are not alone in our struggle. People outside are also working and we now understand that better. We have found some unity. People from the outside can take this experience back to their organizations and use it.

William: The glamorous, exciting thing about it is meeting real people from the outside. At first I was really tense. In here you often think "what's the use?" This class has motivated me. Reminds me that there are people out there who care. Intellectually it has been important too. But it is just so good to remember there is reason to care.

Pedro: This has been a Pandora's Box. It released hope. I know what I want to do, but how to do it? This has made us think.

Theodore: This class has made me more aware politically. Democrats and Republicans are the same thing. At San Jose State [He received confirmation of his acceptance for Fall '71], I plan to study politics—not to enter it but to know how to use it for *La Raza*.

At this point Theodore read a paper he had written—a statement of his transformation from one who looks to himself for explanation of failure to one who looks to the system and its failure to meet his needs—his

Arthur's Journal (cont'd.)

precisely as a random-number table defies interpolation: the fundamentally unpredictable, irrational side of human character. This side makes its demands, too. Demands that can be satisfied only by opportunities to engage in behavior that is deviant from *whatever* norms prevail; that are usually looney, frequently anti-social, and occasionally positively evil.

Like Skinner, Fromm is a bit of a prude. He seems to view with some distaste the Freudian concept of sexual license; he is against smoking (not as far as I can determine, on the unimpeachable grounds that it is carcinogenic), drinking, crime, and the journalistic exploitation thereof, comic books and "movie-day-dreaming" whatever that sinister occupation may be. This is, of course, more or less the standard 1954 two-door model list of no-no's, if anyone cares to recall the era of Elvis, ducktail haircuts, juvenile delinquents, grotesquely "customized" Chevies, and ten thousand songs about the agonies of teenage love. Why did Dr. Fromm swallow it whole? If today he followed the prevailing Mittel-Amerika view that dope and Communism are the twin sources of all evil he would be laughed at, and relegated to speaking engagements before noon klatches of Rotarians. Perhaps he did not really believe it, but merely echoed it by reflex; certainly his penetrating analysis of alienation in modern industrial society reflected no corruption by prevailing social dogma. I would also mark against Dr. Fromm his incredibly naive assertion that criticism of the existing system is welcomed in the United States. What Dr. Fromm means is that nobody hassled him for publishing his various works. I suggest his glib optimism about the status of social or political dissenters in the U.S. would hardly be shared by any of the then extant victims of Senator Joseph McCarthy or of the in-

The book *Sane Society* is more the kind of book I like to read. Why? Because it says more about the world today. It talks about mankind and how he is today—like it says who is there to judge man, any man, and say no one can judge the judge. Like when they were asking about the society with everyone acting alike and someone is not the same then the rest of society say that the man is insane. But who is there to say someone else is insane like we having nothing to go on. For example, take what is happening in the world today. Like the white people act one way, the black another, the brown another, and the yellow another. But all of them say the other is insane. The way I see it is that most people think that if they see someone who is doing something in a way different from how they would do it or want it done, then they think you are insane or something. The man, Erich Fromm, who wrote this book I think is looking at life the way it is—like he wrote about education, food and drug acts, mental health, and even Aldous Huxley. That is just a small list of the things he wrote on. What I think is so good about him is that he tries to answer the things brought up in the book. The *Sane Society*—there is so much in this book you just can't write about it. So I'm going to read it again.

Courtney Cain
B-26494 Soledad

Karlene's Journal (cont'd.)

anger and indignation at being denied opportunities and his recognition of himself as part of a whole body of oppressed/repressed and who must work as a body politic to overcome social inequities. His paper seemed to speak to and for nearly everyone in the room.

Ruben Reyna, reiterating much of what Theodore said, speaks about the meaning and significance of *La Raza*.

Sherwin: (talks about the inhibiting quality of prison) This class gives me the opportunity to say things I have been feeling for a long time but have not been able to say because it might get on my jacket. I'd be charged with agitation.

Sherwin makes a plea for solidarity.

Ben: This class has cleared up misconceptions I had about prisons and the people in them. I had no idea how well developed the inmates are, intellectually and politically. You guys in here are more together than most of the groups on the outside. When I was in the Navy out at sea I had a lot of time to do a lot of thinking, but I had never made the equation.

Francisco: (describes his first encounter with the police—caught with booze as a teenager). Cop: "You people [Asians] don't usually get into trouble." We are treated as token whites. Those who are making it are forgetting World War II. [Glosses over Vietnam—Asians killing Asians.] The consciousness in my home has come late—you have asked a pointed question and I must admit that. But it is happening.

Sherwin suggests getting us all together as an integrated political collective and from his comments we quickly organize a plan for working on a job/education referral service: the inmates will organize the Soledad community.

Arthur's Journal (cont'd.)

famous "Blacklist" that for five years held the entertainment industry in an iron reign of terror, or of any of the quaint practices employed in the South to guarantee that nobody spread any seditious notions about racial equality among the nigrah. Re-elect Sheriff Kretzer.

It would be fascinating to talk today with Dr. Fromm. What, I wonder, is his reaction to comic books now—not to Superman and Captain Marvel, but to the Fabulous Four, to Zap and Head Commix? If he objected to tabacco and alcohol in 1954, how does he feel in 1971, about grass and acid? He speaks of the "best of music"; in 1954, that meant the Boston Symphony to the exclusion of Chuck Berry. In 1971, does it still mean something like the Los Angeles Philharmonic to the exclusion of the Airplane? And finally, I am moved to wonder about his reaction to the current sexual mores, or lack of them, among the young: would he accept this phenomenon into his definition of loving?

I was pleased to see that Dr. Fromm recognized the importance to man of ritual. Mercifully he seems to accept this singular human characteristic as an undeniable fact, and does not attempt to probe into its underlying causes—a probe beyond the current state of the psychologist's art. He correctly identifies sporting and fraternal events and patriotic observances as quasi-ritual; his prophetic vision would have been sharper if he had seen as decadent ritual the functioning of many aspects of our cherished American institutions—schools, the entire system of "justice" (can anyone who has ever watched a berobed priest-judge heaping calumny on a quivering defendant doubt that he has witnessed a modern re-enactment of the rite of guilt and expiation through human sacrifice?), foreign policy, even the plastic-coated antics of consumerism (see the Sunday suburbanite lovingly annointing

At any given time in America there are countless interactions of contradiction and struggle. The mis-educated middle class, having been bribed and pacified by the cheapest of tokens—an apartment, a car, and DDT-infested groceries, have condoned by their silence, political oppression at home, and war pillage and plunder abroad, particularly of the Third-World people. It has gotten so funky these days, that free speech is almost suicidal. America's youth and students are being arrested, beat up, shot up, and killed across the nation. What kind of people or things does it take to stand passively by and watch economic principles so vile, cheap, insane, and inhuman: America is no longer a place that I have to question myself about. This is hell and all of my life I have been continually victimized by it. My whole class has been victimized by it. Therefore, it is by the laws of nature that I stand in irreconcilable contradiction with it. My life is dedicated to the establishment of a new and human order based on reason and love of and for man universally.

Sherwin Forté
B-21899 Soledad

Karlene's Journal (cont'd.)

Sherwin and Roberto Arras agree to work together, with the Black and *Chicano* groups.

Eugene: This is a communal struggle—progressive people uniting against a common enemy. Coming to this class has impressed on me the need for a concerted effort.

Ralph: The problem of people communicating with others of the same skin pigmentation—Is that not the same as at UCSC? Is there any more brotherhood and understanding there where communication is supposed to be free?

Phillip: We in Soledad are building pride and unity which we can take back to the streets.

Sherwin: The administration encourages racism to keep as much division as it can. They will take any measure to destroy unity. When we protested at Central for transferring brothers (agitators) the progressive whites and the *Chicanos* were behind us. They met our demands then but they shipped out the organizers.

Roberto: When there is a need for us to come together we *do* come together. I feel sorry for the Anglos because the administration doesn't give them an organization to come together. They have been fucked over, too.

William: If more than four or five of us get together on the yard, the guards come over and bust us up.

Roberto: The *Chicanos* do have to stay together because they have real problems to deal with and so do the Blacks and whites. We have got to get ourselves together first and then unite all together.

Arthur's Journal (cont'd.)

his Impala with essence of soap and holy water!) are, at least in part, depraved manifestations of modern man's unsatisfied longing for ritual.

Finally, I would observe that Dr. Fromm predicts with great accuracy the emergence of the rock culture. A rock concert is a collective artistic ritual, in which the audience, although participating less directly than the performers, is still involved to a degree that completely transcends the usual status of spectator. A rock concert is all of Dr. Fromm's "common dances, choirs, plays, music, bands" and a great deal more: it has conscious ritual content, is deliberately quasi-religious and directly mystical in tone and content. And you can have it in any flavor you want. There are numerous bands whose flavor, even to the incorporation of instruments like the sitar, is Eastern-Mystical; those given to the demonic reverse side of the coin of Christianity may listen to a group called Black Sabbath (more funky than evil, I hear) or anything by the Rolling Stones (one of their best, although least popular LPs is entitled "Their Satanic Majesties Present") who managed something unprecedented at Altamont by incorporating, indirectly, a human sacrifice into their appearance; and Quicksilver's tone poem "Calvary," capturing in music the ecstatic torment and triumph of the crucifixion, carries the message of suffering and salvation as eloquently as anything ever created in the name of Christianity.

Karlene's Journal (cont'd.)

Courtney: The staff tell the whites one thing, the blacks another, the browns another. They want us to kill each other off. Lock us up and kick on us. They're freaks or something.

Michael: In organizing a strike we unified the entire population. We went to each of the ethnic groups. Many whites were behind us from the hippie/radicals who have joined the progressive movement. Our solidarity showed the staff that it is no longer a racial question. Since that demonstration there has been no more "fuck that nigger or that jap"—for those of us who are aware, we're together. Our fight is against the man who is binding us. And the man is running scared. We are going to have another Congressman next week to hear our demands. They are trying to be nonchalant. The coalition is beautiful. This should be an example to organizations on the outside that coalition can happen with those who are really struggling—not just talking. We did it. A month of solidarity of all people. Even in this class—I don't know what you people do—you go your separate ways—but we get together and rap about it—We operate on a smaller scale but we are still in a world and we all have the same oppressor.

Ruben Reyna: Our mind is our weapon. Our minds are strong. We need you people to help us get our ideas to flow.

Ralph: What about the women? There is a conspicuous silence of this minority group in our class. Maybe their strength is their wisdom—to keep silent.

Zena: There is no solidarity. The Merrill College cafeteria with everyone here and there, no contact, hostility. My contact with white people is exhausting and bad—they grin in my face—The problem of social acceptance—you act like your group expects you to act.

About the beautiful brothers on the inside: their minds are free! I consider the class at Soledad the closest thing to my concept of utopian education. I was able to learn about prisons by going to one and talking with the inmates and all I can say about them is that they are honest and beautiful and they think and they analyze things so carefully. They are a credit to the movement and I hope that when they get out they stay honest and don't get caught up in the jive-time movement games being played by so many of us on the outside who need to be, more than anyone else, seriously working.

Debra Walton
Merrill UCSC

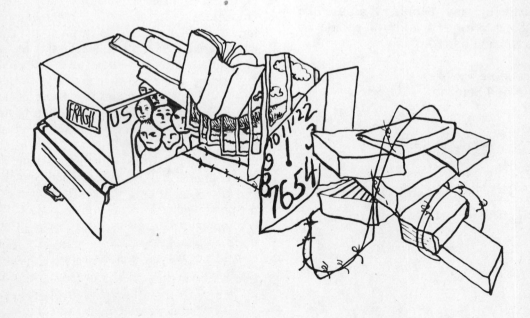

Over the period of 27 years I have lived a broken life for the simple reason that I as a *Chicano*, never took the time to stop and question why I existed in this dog and cat world. But while incarcerated this short period, I have truly opened my eyes to understand the inhuman system that has so mistreated my people. I accuse the U.S. government and its people of racism and hatred.

Theodore Martinez
B-24564 Soledad

Karlene's Journal (cont'd.)

Michael: No one is protecting the leaders. You have to get together. You just put the guys out on Front Street and leave them there. Look at Jimmy Carr and M. L. King.

Pedro: There is still the influence of Gandhi and passive resistance.

Michael: The movement for a lot of people is just a fad.

Before we say goodbye—which today was a series of long, sustained heart-felt hugs and damp cheek-kisses, on-looking guards be damned—Ralph offers a beautiful statement about the effect the class has had on him and the conclusions he has drawn from it about prisons and the necessity for drastic alterations in our perception and application of justice.

I speak about the frustration I feel when the administration boasts of our class as an example of reformist policy when in fact we represent such a ludicrously tokenistic program—how increasingly I'm regarding prisons (and mental hospitals as well) as institutions which enable society to select our unwanted individuals and lock them away to avoid the disturbing challenge which they present to us—how I think it crucial that those of us who consider ourselves to be dedicated to radical change must stop selecting out, exclusively, the Angelas and Newtons and Berrigans and calling them political prisoners and investing our energies in their release while neglecting and often sacrificing the greater masses of imprisoned people who, given their socio-economic inheritances, are just as surely political prisoners.

And so we say goodbye—and drive home in silence.

ESSAYS: A CRITIQUE OF SCHOOLS AND PRISONS

Introduction

Each member of the class selected an aspect of American social institutions as the topic upon which to base his or her final writing assignment. Not surprisingly the choices most often related to either schools or prisons—the parallels between the two institutions had been repeatedly drawn. This section is a collection of excerpts from these papers.

Following the general introductory statements, the section focuses on schools and what might be done to change them. The greater part of the section is devoted to a discussion of prisons and the possibilities for their reform or abolition. The final essay was contributed by Robbie Freeman, who had been expelled from the class by the prison authorities when they learned that she was a member of the Soledad Defense Committee.* (See Journal, April 21.) In a relatively brief essay Robbie has given us an excellent summary and analysis of the Black Experience within the American penal system.

The prisoners within the class contributed more than their fair share of the writing in this section, which seemed remarkable to us given the difficult conditions under which they had to write. Arthur Stasney describes those conditions as follows: "The inmate members of the class face a serious constraint on their efforts at composition. Free members of the class may gain an appreciation of this constraint by locking themselves in the utility closet of a boiler factory, and writing their papers amidst the clamor and knocks of mop handles. Research in this sort of isolated bedlam involves the act of writing off the top of your head while holding your ears." Prisons do not offer the kind of peace-giving solitude which the Quakers had in mind when they promoted penance via solitary confinement. (penance = penitentiary) There is the constant barrage of sound that comes from the clicking of hard heels down long corridors, the chorus of loud voices demanding acknowledgment, the assault of loud-volumed television sets, the jangling of keys, the popping of electric doors, the intermittent intrusion of sirens and bells, and the sweet and raucous sounds of music. Perhaps even more disruptive than the noise was the fear which each prisoner lived with as he attempted to state honestly his criticisms of his environment. Together with the prisoners I experienced continual relief as each week I succeeded in leaving Soledad with their papers tightly in my

*Soledad Defense Committee was comprised of a large number of citizens and attorneys throughout the state of California who raised funds and provided support for the defense of George Jackson, John Cluchette, and Fleeta Drumgo who were charged with the death of a guard at Soledad, January, 1970. ED.

grasp; we all realized that in the event of a shakedown their writings could be confiscated and they could be harshly punished for having communicated their thoughts to us in writing. This fear almost certainly had the effect of subduing the men as they formed their concepts for the essay assignment. Unlike the bold and revolutionary language that erupted spontaneously from them in our discussions, the essays for the most part are tightly reasoned and carefully reserved statements. Their proposals for the restructuring of schools and prisons are reformist and practical, suggestive of realistic change rather than radical overthrow. They write from a framework of the inevitability of our institutions, asking only that these institutions allow for the affirmation rather than the degradation of the human beings who occupy them. The exception to this unexpected position is Michael Lee's serious analysis of revolutionary struggle.

Assembling the material for this section was the most difficult part of the project, due largely to the voluminous quantity of material that had been submitted. In order to avoid extreme redundancy it was necessary to do considerable cutting and rearranging of the original papers. It was necessary to omit some of the papers altogether in order to retain thematic continuity. However, with a few very minor exceptions, the original work did not require editing for structure or grammar. As editors we concentrated strictly on selecting essays or portions of essays which would provide the reader with a balanced representation of the writing from the class.

K. F.

THE SYSTEM

The prison and education systems are really one system. Both institutions degrade and humiliate the person and do not allow importance to anyone. Both exist for the protection of society and its property. Both institutions have tracking systems according to race and class. Both are used for stabilizing labor and for branding inmates. The oppressiveness of both ultimately justifies the use of violence for their overthrow.

The social function of the prison is prevention of crime; the prison protects the other institutions of society. The schools serve similarly. To keep the students off the streets so they don't bother the businesses. If damage is done by degradation, humiliation, moral indignation or by attitudes, then it is psychological violence. Physical violence has been alleviated, but in its place is increased mental coercion. Threat is a method of social control. In prison it is the threat of being sent to the hole, shock treatments, or being sent to the captain. The student is threatened with the principal's office, given the paddle or expulsion.

Psychological violence is the unknown, the uncertain, the institution's ability to enforce isolation. After arrest, the person is isolated from the rest of society. He receives only information which the authorities give him. Students also receive only the information their schools give them.

When a student enters school the first thing he or she does is to count the months, weeks, days . . . left in school. The inmate does exactly the same thing. This is institutionalized uncertainity. Both are put out of a time sequence because of their isolation from society.

The prison administrator tries to make the inmate admit guilt. Degradation and humiliation do not help the prisoner withstand the process of repeating that he is guilty. This repetition is a rape of the mind, a battle for the mind. The schools as well as prisons are institutions of brainwashing.

When a student passes to another grade with a bad record, the student is already degraded before entering the new room. The same is true of the inmate. The moment he enters it begins. The moment he walks out the prison gate, his record will follow him everywhere.

Students are tested and sorted accordingly into special classes and vocational programs. They thus can be treated as second-rate and non-intelligent according to how the institution has programmed them. Likewise, prisons segregate and categorize inmates.

Both inmates and students try to make these institutions as bearable as possible, and make the application of force unnecessary. Thus the system's threat of punishment pays off. The effect of the pressures and frustrations are lessened in the students' and inmates' acceptance of the institutions as places where they must stay for some time. Both institutions want to create this dependence rather than independence.

The frustration of the prison and school life makes both victims release their frustrations at the expense of others. The fear of punishment causes both students and inmates to blame other students and inmates for infractions of which they have been accused.

Education is a tool for conformity and docility; it is one of the most powerful systems of social control and one to which individuals are forced to submit. Schools like a student who will do what the school desires.

Of course, schools do not compare to prisons in the degree of physical or psychological violence that is done to the individual. But in its own way the school demoralizes the individual. The student feels imprisoned because he or she must be there all day until school lets him or her out. This is not total imprisonment, but it is a trap and it can be a transition to the more severe institution of treatment—the prison.

When the inmate gets out on parole, he carries to the outside every aspect of that prison. The inmate might move about physically but mentally the immobility acquired in prisons is carried outside.

The prison and school want to pacify inmates and students. However, they are only making their victims angrier and more aware of their oppression. By learning how the system works, both groups will use this awareness and the skills they have learned against the system that degrades them.

Alma Cota
Crown College, UCSC

AMERICAN EDUCATION

Try to imagine what happens to Juanito. He is fed into the economic-oriented machine that wants to grind him out and assimilate him into a respectable, law-abiding, suburban citizen named John. Juanito hears, "Do this. Don't do that! Love God and your Country." This is basically what he might hear at home, but the concepts are completely different. At the same time, he hears about the pot of gold at the end of the rainbow. He gets a tantalizing glimpse of *la dolce vita*. With everyone pushing him, apparently in this direction, he knows what he's missing, and since he doesn't have the training to do it "properly" he turns to the only ways open to him. He either turns to dope to hide the frustration and for a few hours at least to experience the good life, however false it may be; or, if he can't escape it, he tries for the quick buck by robbing, burglarizing or selling dope. While he's trying to make it in school, he sees *Myron Silberstein* coming to school in his mom's new Oldsmobile stationwagon, eating steak sandwiches and generally having an easy time of it without earning one bit of it. Is it any wonder that Juanito feels fed up, bitter, and at loose ends?

If we can have a sympathetic white man, concerned teachers, and schools where you can truly learn, we'll be well on our way to intellectual freedom. Let's get on with it. We need people with experience or training in the very fields which the elite use to keep us down, i.e., economics, politics, communications. There are many Third-World people who might be somewhat concerned, in however limited a way, with these endeavors. If we can get them to impart their knowledge to us, we can meet the enemy on an almost equal basis. I realize that the above statements make some of our people look like Uncle Toms. Unfortunately, we do have a lot of brothers and sisters who are *white-washed*. These, though, are the people we need now. They give us an entry into the Anglo-American society. We've got to work insidiously in order to keep the structure intact for us when the white rats begin to leave the sinking ship. We also need to train people who are able to run the complex ship of state.

As well, we must convince our people that all the drug cultures are just capitalistic tricks to keep us all doped up so that we don't want to fight and indeed can't fight. How can a person in his drug-induced utopia, think about the cold-bloodedness of the Anglo-American? This is a program of utmost importance. If we can make ourselves get into the Cause wholeheartedly, we won't need drugs!

Pedro Chacon
B-8747 Soledad

AMERICAN EDUCATION

Teachers are supposed to know about all the world's history and not just U.S. history. Like you've got more than just the white race in school and I know that the other races would want to know their people's history, whether it's good or bad. I used to feel that when people wouldn't tell me the whole story, they left something out because they were afraid of something they had done and didn't want anyone else to know what they had done to him or someone he loved. And that's the way I feel about history. They (the people who run the U.S.) are afraid to let the people know what they have done to them and what they are still doing to them. I know that there will be a lot of people or so-called teachers who will not give a damn if the child learns or not; but I also know that we the people can tell if someone is for real or not.

Courtney Cain
B-26494 Soledad

AMERICAN EDUCATION

Being Black myself, and having gone through the California public school system, I feel safe in stating that much of the material taught is outdated, slanted, and irrelevant, especially to minorities. I consider myself one minority student out of many who was adversely predestined by the tracking system. I started out in the accelerated reading group, because I was taught to read before entering school. I was later put into a lower reading group because the teacher disliked my attitude toward school. All through high school and junior high, my schedule on my counselor's recommendation was loaded with general and business education courses. For a while they really had me thinking that I wanted to be a secretary. I never conceived of myself going to college, until one of the few concerned counselors at my high school recommended that I apply to UCSC under EOP, a program for low-income minorities with potential. Looking back on my days at Santa Cruz High, I remember most the unfair disciplinary tactics and the lack of concern on the part of most teachers and administrators that made high school a useless and almost unbearable academic ordeal for me. I've been through twelve years of the public school system, and the only things I consider valuable are the things I learned on my own—because they were of interest to me.

Debra Walton
Merrill College, UCSC

AMERICAN EDUCATION

The Education System in the State of California is a failure as I, a *Chicano,* see it. I emphasize *CHICANO* because my views will most likely differ from other people's who are not of *La Raza.*

A *Chicanito* (small boy) or a *Chicanita* (small girl) has problems from the moment he or she enters the public schools in kindergarten. Not the regular problems most boys or girls encounter, such as being exposed to a new world with children who are total strangers to one another—but problems with communication. Communication with teachers mostly. In 19 out of 20 cases the teachers are Anglos and the problems start there. Don't read me wrong. I don't mean to say the Anglo teacher is incompetent to teach, but that the Anglo teacher does not have the competence to teach a *Chicanito.* This competence I'm referring to is that the Anglo teacher is not hip to the ways of a *Chicanito* or *Chicanita.* In order to teach a child you must first know who he is, particularly in teaching a *Chicanito,* because he has his own Culture and Language that is very different from the Anglo and when a *Chicanito* and an Anglo teacher first meet, there is an instant barrier which prevents communication.

The needs that are so essential to a *Chicanito* are not met by the schools—special needs that the education system is ignorant of. When communication and needs of a *Chicanito* are not met, the teachers automatically reject the *Chicanito* and classify him as retarded or unable to learn. This is the most absurd assumption in the whole school system, yet this sort of statement is made and recorded.

Keep in mind that the *Chicanito* is barely in grammar school when he is subjected to this kind of treatment. Even though he is not told, he is wise enough to know that he is not doing what the teacher has *explained* for him to do. He therefore starts doubting his capability and it is at this crucial stage that the harm (notions of failure) has been inflicted. From then on it is almost always downhill, as far as an education for a *Chicanito* is concerned. The *Chicanito* has only one alternative at this stage: He says just "fuck it." (He still goes to school most of the time, because the LAW says he must until he is sixteen years old.) On top of all this he is still confronted with his parents who always complain because he is failing in school. They tell him why he is failing, plus kick him in the ass for not learning what the "sweet ol' lady" has tried so very hard (that's what Miss Smith tells his parents) to teach. There are many more reasons why I think the Education System is a failure, not just to *Chicanos*, but to Black and Anglo children too. But I feel more for my *Raza* because I can identify with them more readily and therefore give my reasons, as a *Chicano*, first. *Que Viva La Causa.* In recreating the education system, we must first review in depth and destroy the present structure to see that the needs of everyone, regardless of race, creed, or color, are met. As it is now, the education system is DESTROYING the minds of children, which in time knowingly or unknowingly helps to cause more destruction to this already *sick society*. I say "sick society" because it is obvious that something is wrong—that things are not as they should be. A few changes in the system would immediately uplift the spirits and the education of minority peoples as well as young Anglos. For instance, increasing the proportion of minority teachers in all schools, especially in barrio and ghetto schools. Recognition of the importance of the materials used in motivating children; *Chicano* children would find school much more interesting if they were taught their history as well as the fables of George Washington. Parents should be exposed to the schools; they should be encouraged to talk with and about their children in organized meetings with other parents, children, and school personnel. It is indecent the way the educational system is presently functioning and hopefully some changes will be made very soon.

Roberto Arras
B-24050 Soledad

AMERICAN EDUCATION

The atmosphere in our schools today can be compared only to that of prisons. Only in these two institutions can a person be tried and convicted without benefit of counsel, without benefit of a trial by a jury of his peers, or without the possibility of a re-trial. Also, only in these two institutions can a person be forced to conform to certain standards or else. At least in free society if the standards of those around you are unsuitable to your tastes, you are, theoretically, at liberty to move away. A child in school and an inmate in prison do not have that privilege. They are denied the right to think and act as they please, even if what they are thinking and how they are acting affect nobody, not even themselves, in a harmful manner. It was proven to me that the atmosphere in school is comparable to that in prisons when I entered the prison. It took me only six months to adjust to this new atmosphere.

Stanley Mayabb
B-24715 Soledad

AMERICA'S COURTS, PRISONS, AND POLICE

To tell the truth, I think the police are the lawbreakers and that the public has got to protect themselves from the police or they will kill us all off—black, brown, white.

If you've done wrong and you've got money, then you're going back on the street. You know they will let you go. But if you didn't do anything wrong or you did, and you don't have money, then you are going to jail. Like they say, justice is blind. The only reason they don't want you to know the real reason for the blindfold on the statue of justice is that under the blindfold are dollar signs for eyes.

The general public has never evidenced an interest in what goes on inside prisons except when a serious incident (a riot, a mass escape) shatters its apathy. And then the hue and cry is usually for better security. The public primarily demands that things be run with a tight hand; no riots, no escapes, no foul-ups.

Most inmates know that a prison riot is not just a bunch of grown men "raisin' hell" though it is surely that in part. A prison riot is the ultimate tactical resource available to inmates who want to force change. Meaning: the riot is a costly weapon for cons to employ. It may mean loss of lives, it surely means loss of privilege, and it means extension of prison sentences for some involved. But the important thing is that it works. It is the one sure-fire way to force the authorities to reform the prison, because it's the only action that effectively calls attention of an apathetic public to the serious ills of the penal system.

What the public invariably reacts to is the imminent threat posed by a serious breach of prison discipline. "My God," says the fearful homeowner, "what if those dangerous beasts escape from their cages, we may all be killed!" Inmates of America's prisons are escaping constantly, not just in occasional, furtive climbs over high stone walls—but everyday and night by the front gates. More importantly, it is not just a small band of dashing, mad-cap criminals, who "break into the open." The overwhelming majority of prisoners get out—legally. The point then is this: what happens to the man while he is in prison is of critical importance. If he is embittered and brutalized, we are in trouble. If he is helped and changed, we are in luck.

Most inmates will tell you this. "Man, let me tell you, when you come out of a place like this, you hate everyone. You feel like you've been stomped on, and you're going to get back." Most prisons have brutalized, embittered, and dehumanized inmates and then, according to the rules of our justice system, released them back to the public to wreak their vengeance. "All society shows the convict its ass and expects him to kiss it," writes Eldridge Cleaver. The convict feels like kicking it or putting a bullet into it.

They are not apologizing, nor are they asking for understanding; they are warning us. Clearly, they and most cons consider the wrongs accorded them by society to equal or outweigh their crimes. Anyone who has seen no matter how briefly the life they must endure for having taken someone's money, must agree. Society pays for the wrongs done to them as surely as society has made them pay. They will be coming back to society—meaner, tougher, more learned in the ways of the criminal. This is their warning delivered without bombast, but with the deeply cool, ironic humor of men who have come to live with an abomination not by condoning or condemning it but by understanding it.

They write of a criminal justice that accuses men of irresponsibility in the "free world" then consistently denies them self responsibility while in prison and finally releases them with the admonition that they better have learned responsibility.

They write of a system that condemns the brutal act of a criminal, then brutalizes the inmate with physical, verbal and psychological abuse, and smugly warns, "That ought to teach you."

They write of a system that takes abnormal men who have committed abnormal acts and places them in the most abnormal of societies to teach them to be normal.

They write of a system that takes them, the young, 18 and up, the disadvantaged and socially underdeveloped, provides them with none of the psychological and social treatment they so desperately need, then labels them "cured" when their sentences are complete.

The American criminal justice system is unjust, and it is a failure to boot. By its brutal, punitive ethic and its lack of truly corrective measures, the system probably does more to foster crime than to hinder it. Yet despite the public's deep-seated worry over the growth of crime, it's practically impossible to discover strong public support for reform of the penal system.

Perhaps this paradox can be explained only by the fact that people want it that way. Society needs the prisons because they need someone to punish, to scorn, to vilify as the identifiable sinner in their midst. We are all sinners, and as such we identify with the crime. It's natural, then, that we identify with the punishment as means of expiation.

And the con, not surprisingly, is like everybody else. Society wreaks its vengeance upon him. They make him go to prison. And he will wreak his vengeance upon society. Like the good book reads, an eye for an eye, a tooth for a tooth.

Courtney Cain
B-26494 Soledad

THE INDETERMINATE SENTENCE

In the French Penal Code of 1791, a method of punishment was adopted that emphasized the equality of punishment for every crime committed according to its seriousness. This method was called the definite-sentence system and was a product of classical criminology. Again as in the past, the primary aim of this system was deterrence by punishment. In very few instances did it persuade the offender from going out again and committing the same crime or another crime. It was discontinued twenty years later because of its rigidity and modified in the Code of 1810.

Archbishop of Dublin, Richard Whately, in 1832, wrote a letter to one of his colleagues in which he was quoted as saying, "It seems to me perfectly reasonable that those whose misconduct compels us to send them to a house of correction should not be again let loose on society until they shall have given us some indication of amended character . . . "[1] This was the first expression of the theory of the principle of the indetermination in the sentence to imprisonment for the purpose of taking into consideration the rehabilitation of the prisoner. Whately's notion is considered by many scholars of historical penology to form the basis of the much admired system of discipline of Irish prisons under Sir Walter Crofton. The Irish system was the first penal system to declare as its main objective, rehabilitation of the prisoner. This was accomplished by placing the prisoner's fate, as much as possible, into his own hands. In 1866, Gaylord B. Hubbell, warden of Sing Sing Prison, visited Ireland for the purpose of investigating the operation of the Irish system. He was greatly impressed and recommended its introduction into New York. A proposal was prepared by Dr. Wines and Theodore W. Dwight for revision of New York's penal system. After taking an extensive tour of the major penitentiaries in the United States and Canada, Dr. Wines and Dr. Dwight printed a legislative document under the title "Prisons and Reformatories of the United States and Canada," in which they reported:

Whatever differences of opinion may exist among penologists on other questions embraced in the general science of prison discipline, there is one point on which there may be said to be an almost, if not quite perfect, unanimity, namely the moral cure of criminals . . . their restoration to virtue and the spirit of sound mind . . . is the best means of attaining the repression and extirpation of crime; and hence that reformation is the primary object to be aimed at in the administration of penal justice . . . Not a few of the best minds in Europe and America have by their investigations and reflections, reached the conclusion that time sentences are wrong in principle, that they should be abandoned and that reformation sentences should be substituted in their place.[2]

In 1869, Z. R. Brockway, superintendent of the Detroit House of Correction, a municipal prison, secured the enactment by the Michigan legislature of what became known as "the three year law" which is generally referred to as the first indeterminate sentence act. Interestingly, it applied only to women convicted of prostitution and provided that the convicted woman be sentenced to the Detroit House of Correction for a term of three years and that she might be released, absolutely or conditionally, upon reformation or marked good behavior.

By 1895, Massachusetts and Illinois had substituted the indeterminate sentence for the definite sentence to their state prisons. These were the first acts applying to state prisons or penitentiaries. However, both states provided that the sentencing court should fix a minimum and maximum term as provided by state statute. By 1922, thirty-seven states had some form of the indeterminate sentence. The six basic forms of the indeterminate sentence as implemented by these states are as follows:

1. The maximum term fixed by the court in the sentence could not exceed the maximum prescribed by the state statute for the offense.

2. The court had to fix in the sentence a minimum term which shall be the minimum prescribed by statute for the offense and a maximum term which shall be the time fixed by the jury.

3. The court may fix in the sentence a maximum term as prescribed by statute for the offense and a minimum not less than one year nor more than one-half the maximum.

4. The court may fix in the sentence a maximum term not to exceed the maximum prescribed by statute for the offense and a minimum prescribed by statute for the offense.

5. The court may fix in the sentence a minimum term within the limits prescribed by statute for the offense, but no offender could be detained beyond the maximum prescribed by statutes for the offense.

6. The jury could fix a maximum and minimum in the verdict within the maximum and minimum prescribed by statute for the offense.

The use of the indeterminate sentence increased until about 1925, decreased until about 1940, and now is on the increase. At present all but ten states and the federal government have indeterminate sentence laws.

When the time of release is set by an administrative board and the court merely imposes the minimum and maximum limits of the penalty, the sentence is known as an indeterminate sentence. Theoretically, the sentence is not indeterminate, for it has been previously set and should be called indefinite rather than indeterminate. No state has sentences that are completely indeterminate.

It has been the practice to use the indeterminate sentence along with a system of parole. "Parole" refers to the fact that a portion of the period of custody is spent outside of the confining institution. A person on an indeterminate sentence may be released with conditions on parole or without conditions and completely without parole. Originally, not all prisoners in the state that have adopted this system were held on the indeterminate sentence. It had always been the practice to restrict this method to only certain classes of offenders. It generally did not apply to misdemeanors or to serious felonies. It has sometimes been restricted to those above or below a specified age. The restrictions have always been based on the assumption that certain categories of offenders should be punished rather than treated. There is still a prevalent assumption that certain classes of offenders will not respond to treatment. However, in recent years, the tendency has been to extend the indeterminate sentence law to all classes of offenders.

The arguments against this system most frequently presented are as follows:

The indeterminate sentence takes into account nothing except the rehabilitation of the prisoner, while other things, especially retribution and the deterrence of potential criminals should be considered. It is time that society realized that punishment as the shortest road to rehabilitation is not the right road. Usually behind what society does to an offender is the desire for revenge to someone—and the unknown villain proved quietly of wrongdoing is a good scapegoat. Society calls it a desire to have justice carried out, i.e., to have him punished. But these are usually vengeful feelings directed against a legitimized object. There have been many studies that have shown that punishment does not accomplish the purposes by which it is justified.

Thus far there is no satisfactory method of determining when a prisoner is rehabilitated. The administrative board who determines when a prisoner has been rehabilitated in California is called the California Adult Authority. The procedure they follow in determining rehabilitation is as follows:

Advance studies of the cases to be reviewed are not made; they argue that the information on a man is fresher when read just prior to seeing him. The members usually work in panels of two, one man studying the next case while his partner quizzes the inmate before them. They have the assistance of a concise two-page summary of the salient facts prepared by the professional staff.[3]

Finally, the uncertainty regarding the time of release causes much anxiety for prisoners. Some prisoners have stated they prefer a longer term fixed in advance to a shorter term with its early period of worry and anxiety while they await a decision or setting by the parole board. The anxiety created in prisoners is one of the true difficulties of the indeterminate sentence system which cannot easily be overcome.

Joaquin Castro
Cowell College, UCSC

PENAL REFORM: SOME PROBLEMS OF PRISONS
AND POSSIBLE SOLUTIONS

After over fifteen years of delinquency, drugs, crime and prisons, I have come to understand the difference between debilitation and rehabilitation. After too many years of playing victim, I am now able to see with an eye of truth that the increased use of legal detention has paralleled the growth of urbanized lower-classes.

For several years I was led to believe that the acquisition of some of the comforts of home was a giant step toward penal reform. This included such things as: musical instruments, record players, carpets for the cell floor, and a number of niceties from the outside. It was only recently that I came to understand that these were merely new forms of control and pacifiers, which have nothing to do with the resocialization of an individual, and the restructuring of an abused and tattered life. As the penal system exists today, there is little done in the interest of the inmate. After maintenance and processing, care and treatment of a man/woman committed to an institution is next to none at all.

A typical commitment begins with the sentencing of the individual to what the law prescribes. In some instances, the judge and court-appointed functionaries don't even know what it is they are doing when they commit a man to prison. In all probability there are some who sincerely believe that they will, by sending a man to a "training facility," play a significant part in making a contribution to the man in question and to society. Not to mention the wheeling and dealing that goes on in these courts; wheeling and dealing with a man's freedom in order to save the court time. Again, later for the man in question.

On being committed to the Reception Guidance Center (RGC), the process begins to take effect. Medical examinations, interviews and a plethora of processing and other activities overwhelm the "fish" who hasn't really come to grips with the fact that he will be locked away from society, his family and his loved ones for years to come.

Intelligence tests, mechanical tests, reasoning tests, psychological tests, and just about any other test you can name are presented to a man in an organized, impersonal, matter-of-fact process. This is all done immediately. One does not have a chance to come to grips with the gravity of the impending separation from everything that might be near and dear to him. One is not allowed to settle down and perhaps brush up on a subject prior to being administered any of the academic tests, even though the results will determine what level of programs will be made available to the man later on in his sentence. For the most part the Guidance Centers are really only junctions— serving to dispatch men to the institutions which might have *bed space* available, rather than the programs which might benefit a particular individual best. There is a subtle, consistent ever-present reminder of the superiority of the administration. A man becomes de-personalized and is reduced to the status of a number—the emphasis being placed (by those in authority) on passive resignation . . . *control*. Resist not. Submit to fate.

As the system is currently structured, a man must relinquish all responsibility and desire to be a man. Dissent is futile. The quest for self-discovery and individuation is discouraged and thwarted. Sadness and pacification is the tone of life. Routine and regimentation the order of the day. After a while, one begins to think that everything is pre-destined or ruled by capricious forces. Without the capacity at least to influence these forces, one can rarely gratify either hopes or wills. And at the appropriate time one is paroled as a social invalid, unable even to begin to cope with society on even ground. Paternalism and individual responsibility are opposites. The capricious forces which determine "the appropriate time" are commonly referred to as the Adult Authority Board. Under the indeterminate sentence of California, paroles are issued by an omnipotent board of men who ascertain whether a man is to be released or whether he will remain in prison—on the basis of a brief hearing at which data is made available to them by the prison staff. This is a system of much controversy, in that it allows the Board to function without any means of checks and balances. They are an autonomous entity which gives them the status of potentates with the fate of over 25,000 men in their hands—a job and responsibility too large and heavy for a panel of fifteen men with unchecked power. Adding insult to injury is the procedure known as Re-fixing of Time: When a man is granted a parole his term is fixed at a given number of years, e.g., three years in prison and four years on parole. Term Fixed At (TFA) seven years means—or should mean—that at the end of the seven year period, one should be discharged, providing there are no additional convictions. It doesn't work like that at all. Once on parole the parolee is assigned a parole officer. The parole officer serves as the establishment/authority figure on the outside for the continued effect of control—only a bit less physical. At any time the parole officer may violate the parole of the parolee, at which time the parolee can be and usually is returned to prison, *and the sentence automatically reverts back to the original commitment just as if a man were just beginning.* Instead of seven years as the TFA stipulated, the sentence is the maximum (e.g., 5 to life, it's back to life.)

Again I stress the system of unchecked power of this panel of men. And as unpleasant as the thought may be, it is scandalous to think of what happens when politics and public opinion, usually uninformed, are in favor of *law and order.* The compiled data which accompanies a man to the Board is for the most part the result of a ten-minute interview with what is referred to as a Counselor. And the average time devoted to an inmate by his "counselor" is 75 seconds per month.

Mr. Risher is found guilty of robbery and sentenced to prison. The victim of the robbery thinks the punishment will serve him right. Mrs. Risher hopes this time Richard's imprisonment really will give him time to think over the error and tragedy of that kind of life, and that he will go straight when he is released. The Guidance Center Counselor hopes and suggests that Richard learn a trade while in prison that will equip him for a life in society. No one knows (or seems to care) exactly what Richard thinks . . . And with the almost total lack of meaningful guidance counseling, Richard is destined to remain on this treadmill of recidivism for some time to come. Myself and every other offender (political prisoner inclusive) who has received a period of imprisonment has done so because something either within ourselves and/ or within our environment has caused us to be charged with an offense against society. Without attempting to allocate blame anywhere, but merely to follow through a rational process, it is clear that something somewhere needs to change if the offense is not to be repeated. By and large, our environment and society does not and will not change a hell of a lot on its own— either we change that environment or change our attitude and relationship to it.

The emphasis is traditionally placed on the inmate's formative past with hopes that things will change sometime in the future. The present goes unattended. In prison man is haunted by his past; the present is never utilized; and the future hardly ever materializes. Many people working in prisons have at least some good intentions; if only to assuage a guilty conscience. However, they just aren't equipped to understand on a grass-roots level the special needs and complex changes of a man committed to spend some valuable years of his life in prison, or the compulsive recidivist. A better approach to the problem of social reorientation is the peer-group counselor. This involves utilizing people from the community to work with other people in the community; prisoners to work with and assist other prisoners and so forth. We can help each other and assist the caseworkers in defining and interpreting the problems and emotional barriers which accompany a man to this very cold environment. It is well known that the peer-group principle of communication and social relations produces far better results especially when dealing with sub-cultures. With the development of some expertise in the area of sensitivity and motivational techniques we, as inmates, could do one hell of a better job than is being done by our official counterparts (prison counselors). With the emphasis shifted to a more realistic and meaningful program we could return a man to his community as an asset, or at least not a liability. Half-way houses and work-furlough programs are definitely a giant step in the right direction, and should be integrated with the peer-group principle of utilizing other convicts and ex-convicts who now have their heads together.

There should be more inter-action between the community and the prisons; people from the communities and inmates in the prison should be communicating (such as in this class). One of the major shortcomings of prisons is the distinct way it removes the offender from the very environment which precipitated his coming to prison, expects him to change and restructure his misguided life and then returns him to the very same environment—which sets him up for a futile and wasteful life on the treadmill of recidivism—a vicious circle that is often referred to as life on the installment plan.

THE INDICTMENT OF THE AMERIKAN DREAM

MAY IT PLEASE THE COURT: We the people would like to declare
that
the Amerikan Dream
has been busted
on the scales of blind justice
Condemned . . .
The Amerikan Dream is a felonious
fairy-tale
cause Amerikan reality
is funky
funky
funky
WAKE UP
Rip Van Winkle + see that the Amerikan Dream
is guilty of
lewd + lascivious conduct against her own peoples
as well as peoples unable to protect themselves.
How iniquitious + inhuman you have proven yourself to be
Amerikan Dream
You have exterminated one people
+ enslaved another. Your soul
is in prison + your soldiers
condemned . . . No joy — No life —
No happiness
Only routine, monotony, technology
+ WAR
No bars hold you Amerikan Dream
yet your people don't flee
A nation of technological
psychological punks
whose heart was destroyed
when you discovered your mind
Driven by machines, life is
denied your young for fear they won't
see the TRUTH of
GAIN + WEALTH
+ CUT-THROAT COMPETITION
Your armed forces,
special forces, + forces of evil which you
perpetrate on peoples
who can't help themselves. All in the name of
CAPITALISM
+ DEMOCRACY . . . ? With your one-eyed monster
+ your two
car family
that spits out tons of
pollutants for me to breathe in
when I'm not blowing smoke from my
Silver Thin . . .
100
Yes you've come a long way, baby
But just like you
We've come a long way too
And beyond this dead wall
of Amerikanism a spirit moves
whose face will conquer the beast
of greed
+ oppressive militarindustrialism
You have become the victim of your victims
Amerikan Dream

You have become too rigid
　　　　　　+ frigid
　　　　　　　　+ stupid
　　　　　　　　　　+ hung up
　　　in your dream to see that the lust for
　　　　　　　　　　　　　life will never yield
　　　to rules and bars
　　　　　　　or to godless
　　　　　　　　　heartless machines
　　　but will free us of the
　　　　　　　　slavery of deceptive oppression,
　　exploitation
　　　　　+ the illusion of your dream.
　　Nothing comes to a sleeper but a dream Amerika
　　　　　　　　　　　　　　+ we are WOKE
　　You are being condemned by your non-sleeping
　　　　　　　　　　　　　people Amerikan Dream
We the people—
　　　　　　in order to establish a more perfect union—
Sentence you
　　　　Amerikan Dream
　　　　　　　to humanism
　　　　　　　　　+ awareness
　　　　　　　　　　　　　+
　　　love +
　　　　　peace
　　　　　　+ revolution
　　　　　　　　+ progressive
　　　　　　social
　　　　　　　insomnia
　　for the rest of your natural
　　　　　　　life . . .

Richard Risher
B-21915 Soledad

PRISONS: UNIVERSITY OF THE POOR

Before going into what I think may be a formula to change the american joints I would first like to share a bit of experience and tell about the punishments inflicted in this place.

There are two types of punishment used here and throughout the other joints and these are physical and psychological punishments. In the state of California, they punish the mind by giving you sufficient time to think about your indeterminate sentence and in the state of Texas they punish your body by hard labor in the fields. So it is that these two methods of punishment are inflicted on the poor people who, while paying for their own crimes, are paying for those of the rich people who have money to buy their justice. *Pintos* are exhibited as the criminals of america while the real criminals are fucking over countries out there in their world. I'm not saying that middle class america isn't here: there are some and they hold the sickest of beefs (crimes), such as rape of a seven-year-old child, killing of parents, and other crimes of this nature.

From my own experience in this institution, the kind of punishment used against human beings (inmates) is inevitable in leaving some kind of traumatic scars within one's mind. Prisoners upon their return back to the world are never the same. Some never knew what homosexuality meant; from lack of sex with a woman for so many years, they were driven to have sexual intercourse with another man. Others that never knew anger and had had a smooth life all the time are today's worst killers—why? Because that is what this joint does to one. That is the kind of rehabilitation we have here. Just the separation from one's mate is such torture that if any psychologist had a bit of the knowledge he claims, he would try to do something about this. But it's not knowledge they lack, what they lack is courage to liberate themselves from the fear driven into them by prisons.

Another way in which prisons are used psychologically on the outside: if a young brother of the Third World refuses induction into their armed forces (which keeps the economy moving, over which he has no control), the first thing he hears is that he's threatened with prison. And from the stereotyped picture imprinted on him of prisons, he knows they are the coldest places in the world where people will fuck him or pressure him into doing things he normally wouldn't do.

So he prefers to join their army and go kill other poor people of the Third World, here in America and in other countries. Why? Because we can't find a way to convince him that prisons are where the rest of his comrades are.

Prison has changed as did the outside world. What used to be convicts of different races fighting against each other and just fucking up are now political prisoners, concerned with what's happening outside and trying to help out not finding a way to relate to the people outside.

* * * *

I propose that the liberal intellectuals of the Third World and specifically those who are educationally oriented, set up a seminar or conference where we would discuss methods of transforming the present face of prisons into a University of the Poor. We would need the assistance of professors, politicians, writers, students, and anyone who thinks he may have something to contribute to this project. We need outside speakers because inmates would rather listen to an outsider than another inmate. (Our blue suits appear to present some psychological barrier.) This project could also bring better communication and involvement with the outside world and vice versa. We need people to get interested in these places and this could be done by starting ethnic programs, films, talent shows, concerts, tutorial services by students from nearby colleges. We should appoint committees to assist people coming out of prison to find jobs and housing and other needs in the free world. One important program which could involve females is drama. And finally we could start working with present opportunities where men from this institution could attend colleges in the free world and come back to prison at night, such as the programs from Hartnell and Monterey Penisula Colleges.

Inmates could offer people from the streets classes in *pinto* life—for example, on the use of drugs. We could form some kind of curriculum from the experiences of these men which may be relevant to people on the streets such as parole officers. Officers could find out more about the men they are dealing with, instead of trying to find out where these men come from through books.

After such involvement and participation from both sides, we could start work on our conference, designing the curriculum and other plans for the University of the Poor. The first steps are essential to find out what we have and what we lack. The final step, after setting up our program, would be to open it to the public, both inside and outside worlds, where everybody could learn from each other and be happy.

The benefits of my proposal would be first to open communication so that separate parts of the Third World could become involved with each other through our prison university. It would also serve as a means of communication between liberals and conservatives, e.g., junkies and parole officers. But the basic idea is to serve as an example of unity for the benefit of the Third World. The experience would encourage, stimulate and develop inmate talents by placing the full responsibility for the coordination of the conference on the inmates. These men would be encouraged to develop their bilingual and bicultural skills and later to utilize them, upon their release, in their own communities. These skills can be an asset to the movement in communicating with other ethnic groups. We would invite Dr. Rafael Guzman from the free world to provide the major coordination from the streets.

Presently I am mainly concerned with the many problems in our *barrios* and ghettos and the Third World in general. In the future we can share what we get here with other institutions and other brothers that need our support with whatever it may be that the University of the Poor may offer.

Respectively submitted by a Soldier of the Poor People's Army,

Ruben Reyna
B-21734 Soledad

PENAL SYSTEM

All I know and feel is the daily anxiety brought about by laws I must obey. As for the people who carry out these laws, I must say that they know their business like clockwork. They will enforce laws by any means necessary and see that offenders are dealt with by the court system. What is the court system? It's a mass supply of leaders that ride on their white horses making sure that you are supposedly receiving your fair trial. But what is a fair trial? Well, if you have plenty of money, you're sure to get off mildly. But if you have none or very little, you're sure to get time.

I took time to speak to a great many inmates about our penal system. I asked the following question: "Sir, if you had the power to change our penal system, what would you do—change it or just do away with all prisons?" We all agreed that something must be done to change the system. The majority ruled that all prisons should be destroyed and that there should be substituted different kinds of institutions—a medical prison, for example, without walls or gun towers. The main problem would be the constant issue of race— between black, brown and white. However, I would segregate by offense, not race. Why? Because I feel it's most important that "hard core" criminals be separated from lesser offenders. Take for example the dope addicts or first offenders. These men are inclined to have a better chance to adapt to change. But at no time must it be forced upon a man to change or to program. I consider programming a form of indoctrination and I am against it. I put in its place individualism and leave the path open to him to accept his present stay and make the best of it. (When I speak of individualism, I relate to the human factor that we all experience in our realization that we are brought into a world of hate and racism. And when we are aware of this we try our utmost to be what we like to be. But due to laws we are forced to keep some of these feelings bottled up and stored away for the distant future.)

We need change and fast. Therefore, we've got to go to the people, and make them realize that we need their support to make those changes concrete and beneficial. It might be my dream, but I truly believe that people are sick and tired of the continuous hatred that keeps them uptight over chicken-shit-bull-shit. They're beginning to demand changes. For example we must be rid of the Adult Authority system. People who decide people's time should be washed down a dirty drain and left to drown in their own self-hatred. In the place of prisons we would build hospitals where men could be treated by psychiatrists, social workers, therapists, and where all fears could be worked out. *Society must realize that offenses against it are done by people who have been mistreated.*

Theodore Martinez
B-24564 Soledad

THE PRISON SYSTEM

The whole process of the system is structured to make the prisoner live in fear of getting more time for not completely conforming to the program; from the day he arrives at the prison he's exposed to inhuman treatment. Beginning with stripping him naked and forcing him to submit to a hideous skin shakedown—"bend over and spread 'em, boy." A convict isn't supposed to have pride, feelings or self-respect. He's treated like an animal, consequently he acts like one—caged and humiliated and stripped of all individual identity. If a prisoner doesn't quickly accept the policy of prison routine he's placed in the "hole," the Adjustment Center, a prison inside the prison, until the officials feel his attitude merits regular prison privileges. Many men spend years in the hole; some go insane; others die there.

Regardless of the individual's offense, personality or personal preferences, the *treatment plan* is the same. Teach him a trade or give him academic training up to the 12th grade. Many men need psychiatric treatment who will never receive it. The prisoner's daily routine becomes so regimented, so regulated, he loses all contact with reality. Many become nameless robots without the ability to think or make decisions. They become institutionalized and stop caring.

The offender already has some type of social problem, regardless if his crime is murder, mayhem or just being indigent. The latter is why the majority of the criminal offenders are in prison today. The prison rules are so petty, so menial, that the prisoner wonders about the sanity of those whose custody he is in. Are *they* not human? Could it be slightly possible that their shortcomings have a negative effect on the inmates? Why do certain guards overlook minor infractions of institutional rules when others bust their asses to see who can write the most CDC 115's (disciplinary reports) in a day? Why does almost every guard have a few inmates that he tends to give more slack to, and special privileges to, and at the same time have a few inmates on his blackball list—that is to say, that he won't allow them extra or even normal privileges? This adds to the amount of bitterness the prisoner contains within himself, compounding the state of confusion.

Inside the walls of prison the weak get weaker and the defectives get worse. Prison has a sick social structure all its own. Ethnic groups always associate with their own race, and within each ethnic group you will find a number of smaller cliques. These groups stick together when there appears to be trouble in the air—race riots, food strikes, work strikes, etc. Some of the men don't associate with any group, preferring to have but a few friends they feel are dependable in time of trouble. And there are a few who stay completely to themselves at all times, no matter what comes down.

If it were up to me to decide what to do with social so-called deviants, I would discharge 60%-70% of those now in custody—drug addicts, property offenders, alcoholics, juvenile delinquents and other such "misfits"—and have the community work with them locally. The average free person must be educated to some degree concerning the hows and whys of deviant behavior. The public needs truly to realize the fact that deviants are symptoms of a serious social disease. In this highly modern, technological space age, where industry is so advanced and we lead the world, the prisons are full of sickness and human waste. It's downright dumb. You and I should both feel ashamed to contribute to this monster, even indirectly. We need changes and we need them now. Every day that passes without progress is doubling and tripling the urgent need for transition. I hope and pray people will somehow snap out of this state of limbo and start dealing with reality. How can the general public believe this rehabilitation shuck? It's beyond me. If the shoe were only on the other foot . . .

William Lute
B-25871 Soledad

* * * *

UNCONVENTIONAL UTOPIA

I've heard a lot of talk lately, about a better way of life
Some people think it can only be achieved by using the knife
    Others feel that we should reconstruct our values
For if we don't change something now, we're sure to lose

    Most Americans are on a trip, they live only for fun
Our capitalistic class structure drives many to pick up a gun
    Sometimes I wonder if what they call "generation gap"
Isn't just a squares' clean-up, for not knowing where it's at

    "Power to the People" is where it's really at
People of all races, we're nowhere without that
    Our faith must include the whole population
Without believing in our work, we'll still hassle segregation

Utopia will be a complex state, in my conception
Yet by the same token simple—there will be no exceptions
We would not have Poverty, Prison, War or Pigs
All men will be brothers, our mutual respect will be big

This unique world will have no place for social taboos
Such as penalizing weedheads when the judge is on booze
Sex would be a personal privilege in everyone's life
No laws carrying 1 to 50 years for oral copulation with the wife

The society I desire would condone the use of drugs
We would not advocate violence, bullies or thugs
In the case of a member continually assaulting his brothers
He would be hospitalized and treated, separate from the others

He would be treated like a man, inside the institution
Being sick doesn't change man's basic construction
His local peer group would determine his treatment
Within a short time he'd be released without resentment

A man is a human being, his body and mind have basic needs
Even animals in zoos have mates, men too need more than feed
What crime is serious enough to charge a human fee?
How many really know how it is to be free?

Utopia is an exclusive paradise, an elite state of mind
It's too perfect a domain for too many men to find
It's almost impossible for us to realistically achieve
But we can improve ourselves, this I truly believe

Riots, wars, crime, poverty, pigs and pollution
It's a fact to many of us that we're on the brink of revolution
So much is wrong, we must deal with the worst first
Like the pig, it's getting so fat, it's just about to burst!

William Lute
B-25871 Soledad

UTOPIA????

Third World people live with the day-to-day uncertainty of not knowing if there will be food on the table, or when the bill collector will come, or how long the welfare will hold out, or whether the gas and electricity will be shut off, or what to do when you get evicted, or what to do if your child is bitten by a rat, or how to keep the roaches and rodents from invading our homes. These are very real problems to the have-nots who live in a society such as ours, where technology means economic security to those members of society who reap the profits from that technology.

Blacks have been the vanguard in the struggle of Third World people in Amerika. Blacks have been in the political arena for centuries. Recently other groups have moved to a level of political awareness that allows Third World people to present an allied Third-World front. The new front helps all members. Third World people are not concerned with dreaming of Utopia, but simply with the on-going struggle for freedom. Third World people may someday be in a position to dream of Utopian Societies but right now politics must be our priority.

Plezena Shack
Merrill College, UCSC

THOUGHTS OF AN ASIAN-AMERICAN

Unity is the foundation of any organization; once unity is disrupted in any way, you no longer have that foundation. People will tend to follow the most stable approach; whether unity is firmly established or not, the people will follow. Most of your followers are people who have been brought up with the principle of security. Whether it be present or future security, this principle is firmly embedded in their minds. Now they grow up, they finally step out the door in a sense, and this one-time sense of security is gone. They don't know where or how to go. They have a feeling of independence, but they still fumble around experiencing and learning. There has yet to be any con-structiveness in their actions. Why?

During the growing-up stage (junior, senior high, first-year college), all this energy has been stored up, all the education they have received is ready to go to work—so they think. All right; they step out the door, actually babies to the outside world, all the various ways of life that they have been taught are found to be alien to what they now see. So confusion and fright set in, they ask themselves, "How do I cope with the present situation?" The solution cannot be found in any textbook and the majority of them won't listen to reason, so they roam. They think they're going somewhere, but actually they're going no where but in a big circle. Because they are confused, they tend to evade reality and fall into the realm of fantasy, which includes drugs and hippie-type sectarianism.

When confronted, they will defend their rights by calling or labelling themselves as Third World type people or revolutionaries. They reject all political action, especially all revolutionary action, they wish to attain their ends by peaceful means and endeavor to do so by small experiments necessarily doomed to failure. And in turn, they become reactionary toward the progressive movement of the people. Stokley Carmichael once said, "many people who want to be revolutionaries, think the dirtier they are, the more revolutionary they are." It must be realized that when armed struggle is evident, it will be "urban guerilla warfare." The insurgent act will take place on the city streets and in residential areas. It seems that everyone is trying to look like Che in Bolivia or Castro in Cuba. I believe that the true revolutionary has not been properly defined: a true revolutionary accepts no recognition for having performed a deed. You don't have to look radical to be radical. True dedication and sincerity comes from within—not from the way you dress or what you wear to identify yourself with a certain group of people. In essence, a true revolutionary is an individual whose total interest and purpose for existence is to help attain total emancipation and liberation of the oppressed peoples.

As Chairman Mao-Tse-Tung states, "the new culture and the reactionary culture are locked in a struggle in which one must die so the other may live." In this country the reactionary culture consists of the bureaucrat-capitalist-imperialist and all its running dogs, who spread inhumane aggression all over the world. The new culture consists of all the peace-loving people of the world, to be specific, all the people of color. We are the oppressed people of the world.

We are peace-loving people, but it is evident that peace no longer exists. It has been torn from our very presence. Through the tyranny and greed of the U.S. imperialists and their puppet allies, thousands of Asian men, women and children are being massacred in southeast Asia. But the NLF and all the other liberation forces will continue to struggle and fight the savage invaders. Liberation will be attained and the Imperialist forces will be defeated, for they (and all their lackies) are paper tigers. It is our duty as oppressed people to support the liberation forces in Vietnam; and as well, all forces fighting the U.S. aggressor. Third-World unity is expressed in this country but in reality it is only rhetoric. There is still division among people of color. Unity must realize that the power is in the people, that although we face a monstrous structure, we have nothing to lose but the chains of oppression. The people of Southeast Asia face the same monster, but they continue to struggle—as Third World people, we must do the same. "As long as there is exploitation and suppression of the people, there cannot be equality."

Bourgeois ideology has played an important role in the alienation of peoples of color in this country. Through bourgeois methods of indoctrination, the family and all its members are transformed into simple articles of commerce and instruments of production. The bourgeois sees his wife as a mere instrument of production. He understands that the instruments of production are to be exploited and naturally concludes that this applies to women. He has not a suspicion that the point is to do away with the status of women as instruments of production. All aspects of man being a "social being" are blocked by the bourgeois mentality, all concepts of love, brotherhood, and equality are nothing but useless concepts, for they do not show profit.

In the United States, we are not faced with the problem of being a rural, backward country. Our crisis lies in the economy. The American revolution cannot be modeled after Mao's China or Castro's Cuba, but we must see their experiences and theories and apply them to our present situation. In this country there is not a standing proletariat; an advanced modern proletariat must be developed of the oppressed peoples. They must form a vanguard to guard the masses, to unite as one, so as to form a striking force to overthrow and totally destroy the bureaucrat-capitalists and to proceed in bringing about social and economical change and the development of a "socialists' America." As long as the imperialist-bureaucratic-capitalists control the key branches of the economy, it is impossible to get rid of their plunder and exploitation. "If there is to be a revolution, there must be a revolutionary party to guide the masses to victory."

To bring about these various conditions, revolutionary violence is a necessity, for without revolutionary violence, the proletariat cannot triumph in the struggle to overthrow the power machine of the exploiting classes and establish political rule of its own. "Political power grows out of the barrel of a gun," Chairman Mao.

So by means of the revolution the proletariat makes itself the ruling class, and as such, sweeps away by force the old conditions of production and power. Then it will, as well, have swept away the conditions for the existence of class antagonisms, and of classes generally, and will thereby have abolished its own supremacy as a class. We shall have an association in which the free development of each is the condition for the free development of all.

As an Asian-American who is confined within the most concentrated form of oppression, I join the struggle for liberation and peace. Let it be known that within and without, the struggle is waged; exploitation and suppression of the incarcerated people is an everyday experience. We have no arms to fight the oppressor, but we continue to struggle, for we shall not submit.

Michael Lee
B-24542-A Soledad

HERE AND NOW; THEN AND THERE

In its attempts to dehumanize and emasculate inmates, the California Penal System has succeeded in raising the political consciousness of a portion of the inmate population. Men like John Cluchette, Fleeta Drumgo, George Jackson, James Carr, and Bunchy Carter are all products of the California Penal System. All of them are filled with hatred and mistrust, hatred and mistrust toward the system which continually works against the interest of the people.

But more important is the fact that these men and those like them are filled with a revolutionary determination to bring capitalistic thingism and its byproducts to a complete and final end: "People who come out of prison can build up the country. Misfortune is the best test of the people's fidelity. Those who protest at injustice are people of merit. When the prison doors are opened the real dragon will fly out." (from *Prison Diary*, Ho Chi-Minh).

Men like those mentioned on both sides of the prison walls are working to establish a new order. A new society based on human dignity and respect. A new order, unfortunately too far in the future to see clearly but one can surmise how it will be.

The New Order is one based on humanism rather than thingism. It is a society which addresses itself to meeting the needs of the people. Unlike today's society, the society of the New Order is one in which the members have a real concern for each other. People have come to the general realization that all members of society have the right to live a decent life and that it is the duty of society to insure this for all its members. Poverty and subhuman conditions of living are not the way it has to be for any portion of society. It is the philosophy of capitalistic thingism which makes racism, poverty, and hate such prevalent aspects of this society. Unlike the present system, the system of the New Order has aimed at eliminating these and other negative aspects of our society. Everyone is insured adequate food, clothing, shelter, medical care, and education. The frustrations caused by poverty have been eliminated and with them the occurrence of crimes committed out of a need to survive. The existing society is such that for poor people of the Third World, survival depends on cunning. If a Third World person in poverty wishes to survive in even a semi-dignified manner, he must assume the role of an illegal capitalist. He must exploit whoever is at his disposal. He's doing much the same thing as the big business owners but his method of acquiring material things is not prescribed by law. The system of capitalism functions in such a way that people view each other as exploitable commodities.

This would not be the case in the new society, due to the fact that everyone would have access to the material and psychological resources necessary to satisfying basic needs. This is not to say that there would be no crime in the new society, but the incidence of crime would be greatly reduced. Some of the basic problems of human nature would still be present. Some individuals would still fall to the temptation of taking more than their rightful share, and there would still be problems of violent crimes committed against others. Such offenders would have to be dealt with in a constructive manner. The majority would be dealt with on a probationary level, others would be sent to treatment centers. The emphasis of the treatment philosophy would be on re-socialization of the inmate rather than on punishment. The inmate would be expected to work in a cooperative way within a restricted community.

The physical structure of these centers would be physically and psychologically appealing and would include both men and women so as to decrease the frustration caused by sexual deprivation. In an effort to make the inmates aware of the necessity for collective work and cooperation, they would raise a large portion of their own food as well as perform all the essential tasks in the running of their community. Inmates would determine what crops were to be raised, how much was raised, and what would be done with the surplus. This collective experience hopefully would cause the inmate to be more willing to take part in collective efforts upon his release.

The center would be under the auspices of a local review board. It would be made up of progressive lawyers, psychologists and concerned and knowledgeable citizens. The board would reflect the ethnic makeup of the center's population. The board would have the duty of investigating inmates' complaints of mistreatment. The staff and administration would also reflect the ethnic population of the center. They would be made up of mentally stable individuals who would undergo thorough psychological examination before being assigned to a job in the center. They would aid in the resocialization of inmates and would be subject to dismissal if complaints by inmates were found to be true. There would be a medical and psychiatric staff to answer to the inmates' needs, and every inmate would receive extensive care. There would be a great deal of formal education as well as extensive vocational training programs. Upon his release, the inmate would be placed in a job position where he could use the skill which he had learned in the center or, if he wishes, he might enroll in college to continue his education. Regardless of his choice, he would be welcomed back into the larger society.

The *here* and *now*: American society where the value of things is greater than the value of people.

The *here* and *now*: A society which is filled with hypocrisy, brutality, injustice, racism, thingism.

To rephrase a statement by Malcolm:

> Don't be shocked when I tell you I'm in prison.
> I've always been in prison.
> That's what America means: PRISON.

The *then* and *there*: A society where all members live in dignity and respect. Void of racism, exploitation and poverty. A humanistic society whose members work collectively for the collective good.

151

We are doing more than just dreaming of it.
We have armed ourselves with creative minds,
love and most of all the desire for freedom.
It is more than just a dream . . .

Eugene Calhoun
Cowell College, UCSC

PRISONS AND SOCIETIES

. . . In contrast to the system of modern law and justice in Nevada and California, it is of value to examine other systems. One system which had a similarity of ideals with contemporary American society was that of the Cheyenne Indian Nation. While in many so-called primitive systems private law outweighs public law, this was not true of the Cheyennes. The bulk of Cheyenne law is public and centers about murder and the promotion of unity. Cheyennes are trained to be militarily aggressive, for which there is reward, to suppress sexual drives and to be individualistic. These values have many parallels and similarities with present-day American society.

American society handles deviance from its norms as expressed by law, by arresting, judging, and imprisoning deviants. Generally imprisonment far exceeds the point of effectiveness in terms of rehabilitation. A murderer in our society could serve a term of life imprisonment or be executed by the state. The Cheyenne dealt with murder in a much more effective and humane way. The murderer was believed to be polluted causing him to "stink." A lifetime of partial social ostracism could be informally imposed. E. A. Hoebel describes the Cheyenne law as follows:

On the legal level, the ostracism takes the form of immediate exile imposed by the Tribal Council sitting as a judicial body. The sentence of exile is enforced, if need be, by the military societies. The rationalization of the banishment is that the murderer's stink is noisome to the buffalo. As long as an unatoned murderer is with the tribe, "game shuns the territory; it makes the tribe lonesome." Therefore, the murderer must leave.[4]

While this banishment seemed cruel in its own way, it was also usually temporary. The Cheyenne so valued individualism and the individual personality that a man could return when the "stink" had left him. This occurred when the man presented himself to the tribe and declared never to put his desires above the tribe's. E. A. Hoebel commented on the individual's return to his tribe:

They therefore work always toward reform and individual rehabilitation. For them, the law is corrective; it is never employed as a vindictively punitive measure. Punishment, in their view, need go no further than is necessary to make the individual see the right. Once they are convinced the knave is reformed, they move smoothly to reincorporate him into the community. After a period of years—three, five, or ten—his banishment may be commuted. At this point the feelings of the relatives of his victim are taken into consideration, for they must consent to the commutation.[5]

The effectiveness of this system is reflected in the study of Cheyenne law by Llewllyn and Hoebel, in which only 16 intertribal killings occurred from 1835-1879.

The Cheyennes legislated law through the "Council of Forty Four" which was composed of members from each of the warrior societies. The societies dealt with matters of immediate urgency by legislating law to cover given situations. If the decision was not fundamentally sound and not accepted by the tribe, it would not remain law. Small matters did not go to the Council.

Since every man belonged to a warrior society or "club," any decision regarding a law violation would be examined by his peers. Even if truly serious offenses were involved and the Council convened, the individual still was represented by his own society, thus insuring peer-group consideration of the offense. In contrast American society tries poor people with juries of non-peer group members, thus ensuring injustice.

In contemporary society the prisons contain people who have transgressed laws dealing with private property. Most laws do, in fact, deal with the concept and protection of private property. Laws against robbery, theft, burglary, embezzlement, and the like are merely a supportive tool to perpetuate private ownership. Contemporary society could learn much from the Native American concepts of private ownership. The Plains Indians held land and its resources communally, thus only personal possessions were privately owned. This eliminated the need for private property laws and the associated potentially dangerous conflicts. On the other hand, the sub-arctic dwellers of Athabaskan and Algonquin groups adapted to capitalism and private ownership without sacrificing tribal unity:

A truly impressive aspect of the adaptation to capitalism and land ownership was how well these Indians maintained the band's traditional cooperation. Trespass was now defined as someone entering another's territory—but only with intent to obtain furs to sell. It was not trespass if he entered another family's territory to fish, to collect berries, or to strip bark from trees for a canoe. The products of the land were still owned communally. Trespass applied only to those items—the fur of beaver and other mammals— that were desired by the white trader.[6]

These concepts avoided the hoarding of wealth and human necessities. The distribution of wealth was thereby assured. Stealing became unnecessary, as did laws and punishments to protect the society from the conflicts of private property ownership.

The methods employed by so-called primitive peoples to deal with law and justice were quite humane and understanding methods. Laws governing the ownership of property and its protection fail to exist in most primitive societies. The conflicts due to laws, judicial systems and prisons are absent in the groups discussed. They are absent because the wealth is distributed and basic human needs are a priority. Until American society redistributes its wealth, provides for basic human needs, and insures the human rights of its citizens, the society's right to exist is questionable. The barbaric, inhumane practice of confining a person for years at a time is absent in even the most primitive societies. Prison supports a society unwilling to provide for its members. The prisons' accomplices are the law enforcement and legal systems. The time is long past to abandon the inhumanistic, cruel state of this government's transgressions against oppression of its own poor and working-class citizens.

Benn Dunn
Merrill College, UCSC

JUSTICE AS MORAL RESPONSIBILITY

We would have a society in which the only means of social control would be the general acceptance of its customs as rules of obligation. Custom would set the standard of conduct and, more importantly, it would make interpersonal respect the basis of conduct within the society.

If, for example, our new society had as its moral rule "that one ought not cause another bad feelings," any offense would not be seen as an infraction of a formalized law but as a breach of interpersonal respect. Retributive action on the part of the offended would be understandable but not morally condoned. Instead, the system would allow for the placing of responsibility on the one at fault. This would internalize the elements of justice. In this system, guilt or fault would be brought about by peer-group pressure and, if necessary, a lower standing in the community. There would not be the need for an institutionalized legal system which legislates, arrests, tries, imprisons and executes. Today's legal system is entirely punitive and punishment does not equal justice.

The elaborate court system would be replaced by a council which would be responsible for adjudicating fault. The individuals who would comprise the council would be men and women from the community who would be acknowledged for their "moral leadership." They would have no special privileges or elevated social position. This would eliminate the business of judgment as well as the apathetic judges who have no contact with the people they judge. It would also eliminate the upper-class, conservative grand juries who come out of the same background as the judges—with the same perspectives or lack of perspectives. It would also eliminate the high-priced attorneys whose efforts for a particular case are based solely on the ability of the accused to pay for his innocence. Instead the accused would be on trial before his peers, since justice would be handled solely on the community level.

Anything higher than the community council would be non-existent. Abstract debates over points of law, through which men and women's lives rest on the outcome of such debates, would cease. Particular cases, as they relate to accepted moral rules, would be the only concern. Legislated laws such as we now have and which in many instances take no account of the individual case and the possible mitigating or extenuating circumstances involved, will fold back into their hypothetical sources. For, clearly, the present system does not concern itself with individuals and this fails to administer justice to the people.

Lawyers and judges would merge into a council whose only goal would be to adjudicate the particular case. The counsellors would not involve adversary proceedings in the conduct of their settlements. Since social and personal problems would be handled amongst the people in the community, there would be no need for a prison or police system. It would be the responsibility of the council to find a just settlement in the best interests of the community, the offended and the offender. Since law and order is not the concern here, police would not be needed. Justice does not require guardians of a class value system since in a totally just system there are not class distinctions.

Finally, since there would be no institutionalized system of laws but in its place a legal recognition of the accepted moral rules, there would not be the development of the two separate systems—one moral and the other legal, as we have them today. Under the present system, rulings by the U.S. Supreme Court are made according to the logic of the law, as that body understands it, but it may and does often meet with moral disapproval from segments of American Society. Rulings of racial segregation, for example, accept integration and de-segregation as legal answers to moral problems. In a just society, such problems would not have come about because racism is morally corrupt and can only grow within systems which themselves are immoral and corrupted.

Conflicts between the morally and legally valid would not occur if moral rules would be the sole source of what we recognize as "legal." Legality and morality would be indistinguishable.

What has been proposed is not entirely new. Much of it is based on the system of the Tiruray tribe in the Philippines. (see Stuart Schlegel's *Tiruray Justice*). Huxley's *Island*, Skinner's *Walden II*, and some of the communes mentioned in *The Alternative*, share parallels: they all advocate a non-dominance of elitist groups which have special privileges, a strong sense of community in which interpersonal respect is the prime concern; and the absence of a strongly structured and institutionalized political/legal system. This of course presupposes that all people are moral, which may not hold true in this society. However, the necessity of developing a morality that encompasses all people and the structure of the system itself is evident.

Francisco Mantua
Merrill College, UCSC

THE BLACK MAN IN PRISON

The Format:

This paper is about the Black man in the American Penal Institution and how his experience differs uniquely from any other group of inmates. My main concern is with what happens inside the prison. The following section (How Does He Get There? . . .) will be merely groundwork, valid, but not deeply treated, to make the body of the paper more comprehensible to the reader who has had no experience even remotely comparable to Black ghetto life and might therefore suffer some difficulty in understanding the facts as presented. The body of the paper (How He Survives Once There) is the essence of what I wished to expose from what I have learned in my visits to prisons and my encounters with Black inmates (and, of course, books that I have read). And the final section is not meant to be a denouement but meant to help explain the problems of re-entry into the society at large for the Blacks and to show that rather than the end of the prison experience, parole can be the beginning of the road to recidivism.

How Does He Get There . . . ?

It seems phenomenal that almost fifty per cent of the inmates in American penal institutions are Black since Blacks constitute only twelve per cent of the entire population in America. Why is it the Black man is so often imprisoned? What causes him to commit five to ten times as many reported crimes as whites?[7] Is it just economics that makes crime such a widely accepted and repeated activity among Blacks? We can clearly see how prison is imminent for a large number of Black individuals in a limited investigation of the environment which nurtures and surrounds them until the time of their arrest: the ghetto.

Of the main components of the Black ghettos, the most germinal and perpetuating factor is the extreme poverty of its inhabitants. This is a poverty caused largely by the hierarchical chain of American institutional policies which have kept the Black man poor since his abduction to this country; kept him menially employed or unemployed. But it is the effect of poverty which concerns us here more than the causes because it is these causes which create the ghetto environment. In 1903, W. E. B. DuBois wrote, "To be a poor man is hard, but to be a poor race in the land of dollars is the very bottom of hardships."[8]

The effect poverty has on a man's self-esteem in a country where "you are what you have" is terribly defeating and frustrating. It means being constantly confronted with the American ethic that one is insignificant and indeed *is* nothing if he has nothing. It is interesting to note that recent studies show that one reason the ratio of Black to white criminals is higher for Blacks is because there are proportionately more Black young people than there are white in each population and it is the young (18-35) who commit most offenses.[9] It is easy to see that it would be the young Blacks who desire more because they, unlike their parents who have been denied the essentials, are imbued with the hope of everything, the resentment of filthy ghetto living creates an ambition in them to progress, "to move up and out" of their substandard communities. When this ambition collides head-on with the systematic and systemic denial which America imposes, the Black man soon learns that there is little hope for that gateway that leads out of the ghetto to be opened by honest, hard work.

But by the time he has probably (at least once) been denied the opportunity to work his way out of the ghetto at a salary compatible with comfortable living for him and his family, the odds are that he has also been denied the education required for the kind of job he needs. 1968 figures show that most Blacks do not finish high school (sixty per cent as compared to thirty-eight per cent white who don't) and only fifty-eight per cent finish the eighth grade (seventy-three per cent whites do) and in college, the scarcity thins to one Black enrollment per hundred whites.[10] While I was in high school in the ghetto (until the tenth grade) I once visited a school in a white ghetto (through some integration program) and I had an opportunity to compare the differences. The main difference (and "a number of experts" have come to the same conclusion) was that the Black school is staffed largely by middle-class whites from sterile white homes and sterile white universities who consider it their duty to teach in the ghetto. They "realize" that the Black child is inherently intellectually inferior (which is why they came to "help") so they teach him as though he were inferior and expect little of him. His tests usually consist of true/false and multiple choice questions which require little thinking. That's the crux of the problem: the ghetto youth is seldom asked to think in school; he is asked to recollect but never to conceptualize. Consequently, he probably leaves high school, whether he graduates or drops out, not prepared to think for himself and with a dependency on someone else for the answers. Most Black students realize that little is asked of them but they "fail in school because that is precisely what is expected of them . . . "[11] Unfortunately, most tenth grade students (of all races) do not look far enough ahead to try and gain as much from high school as possible so they don't complain although they realize that they are being substandardly educated. It is difficult for them to see how much it matters. (I hope you will bear with me as I continue to relate my personal experience as I think it is pertinent to this topic.) When I returned to my ghetto school after visiting a white school and told a particularly patronizing teacher that I was tired of being fed answers to token questions and that I wanted to learn to understand and not just repeat, he seemed to understand. He suggested I tell the rest of the class my proposal for researching answers and discussing concepts to see if they wanted to change the format of the class. They didn't. They dismissed me as being "smart" and had been so indoctrinated to believe themselves "dumb" that they considered themselves incapable of doing what I was going to do and it would be safer to get a passing grade and learn nothing than try something that they had practically been told they couldn't do and certainly had never been allowed to try, and fail. So, although most of them passed the class, I could tell by the final exam that we were all *expected* to know nothing. In the white school, which I transferred to after that experience, all the classes I had differed greatly from those that I took in the Black ghetto school. The teacher gave an assignment and expected it done on a certain date. It was up to us to get the information to do the work even if it was not to be found in the textbook. I began to do work with so much less teacher supervision that I *had* to think for myself. With my ghetto background, I did rather poorly at first, the competition was really stiff, but when I graduated, I did so with a twelfth grade education which is much more than I can say for many, many ghetto graduates.

But where is the incentive to graduate in the ghetto? It is not those in the schools who are "making it"; who "have" and therefore are "someone." Not even those who do graduate because Black males who complete high school make about $5,801 (as compared to the $6,452 that white males make)[12] and that is barely subsistence to the man with a family of four in an urban setting when the Black man pays more for substandard housing than whites. It is invariable that those who were forced by need and/or imbued desire resort to violent or non-violent illegalities for money. The pimp, the pusher, the armed-robber. (In these men the ghetto youth find their heroes because they have money—they are someone.) They can afford to drive, wear and live in what the average ghetto Blacks are all too poor for but have been trained by the mass media to crave. The sociologist M. A. Forslund, though, said that if poverty were eliminated the Blacks still would commit three times as many crimes as whites. This he attributed to the resentment by Blacks at white society, plus a ghetto culture that encourages criminal behavior.[13] This touches on "making it" and the imbued desire to "have" while being repeatedly denied. Because white America has so long refused to recognize the adulthood of Black males, what is important within the culture is be-coming a "man" and constantly proving one's masculinity. Violence is the classic manifestation of authority (which is essential for confirming one's masculinity); this is how some sociologists have partially explained violence in the ghetto. Most add to confirmation of masculinity: manifestation of frustration and resentment of their surroundings and all connected with it. Violence is also a means of defense against the offenders. Offenders are found in all societies; and offenders are found in the ghetto committing offenses to other Blacks, either for reasons stated above, or for more personal ones.

In mid-September 1968, Ramsey Clark testified before the National Commission on the Causes and Prevention of Violence on crime in the ghetto. According to Mr. Clark:

Negroes, twelve per cent of the total population, were involved in fifty-nine per cent of the arrests for murder: fifty-four per cent of the victims were Negro. Nearly one-half of all persons arrested for aggravated assault were Negro and the Negro was the primary victim of the assault . . .[14]

I can offer at least two explanations why the Black man's victims are often Black. First, a man seldom selects the person from whom he steals except perhaps to choose a store, etc., with which he is at least vaguely familiar and the area he is most familiar with is, of course, his own ghetto. Needless to mention, people are often killed in robberies. Second, since violence is applauded in the ghetto by young males (especially) as a show of masculinity and courage, reactions to anger or grudges often take the shape of assault with a deadly weapon. From that action to murder is a matter of chance as much as intention. Third, it has become evident in American judicial history that the penalty for killing a white man is usually much more severe than for killing a Black. For centuries, the general attitude has been to "let them kill each other off" as long as they don't harm any whites.[15]

Criminologist Marvin Wolfgang's theory on what the F.B.I. sees as a new upsurge in Black crime is that the only reason it is so high now is because now that Blacks have moved to the cities crime is reported more. And that when Blacks move in where whites are still living it is reported more than Black crimes against Blacks. He compares it to the slums of Paris and the Left Bank where crimes raged for years but none (or very few) of the "reputable" citizens were victims so that the crime rate there was ignored.[16]

So violence and crime are two of the common responses of many ghetto youth to the disappointment, sorrow and frustrations which must be confronted daily;* but inevitably, for whatever reasons the Black man commits crimes, we find that he is the one most often caught (both literally: by police, and figuratively: in "the system") and he can be assured that the system which helped get him there won't help get him out. The next trap for him is prison. (*See note on next page.)

Some Blacks who respond at all to the oppression do not respond outwardly against the system but inwardly against themselves. There are undoubtedly a number of Blacks who are injuriously self-degrading as a result of believing white America when it says they're no good (although assuredly the number is decreasing). But still, as a result of severe emotional disturbances, the ratio of Blacks to whites committed to public institutions is 2:1. Also, between the ages of twenty and thirty-five, in a representative American city, twice as many Black males as whites kill themselves (whites equal and overtake Blacks in suicide after forty-five because it is then when whites feel they have no future; the feeling comes much sooner in Blacks.)[17]

How He Survives Once There . . .

In this analysis I shall forego a long description of the time between arrest and time of conviction and sentencing. The procedure is the same for all poor people. They are assigned a busy Public Defender because they cannot afford to hire an attorney. The "P.D." advises him to plead guilty because he "hasn't got a chance" and tells him they'll try to get as light a sentence as possible if convicted. He is, of course, convicted (guilty or not). Time magazine exposes one reason why in an article on the lack of respect that Blacks have for the law:

[It is a] truism of American affairs—that a people's respect for law depends largely on the law's respect for them. It is an equal truism of United States life that nearly all Black defendants are tried by white juries, a fact that fuels Black suspicion of "white law" . . . [18]

After conviction, it is most common in California to receive an indeterminate sentence to a "correctional facility." The indeterminate sentence is an interesting one. It is the most manipulative device the legislature has for assuring "good conduct" within the prison. When a man receives an indeterminate sentence (the ultimate is one to life) it means he can serve a minimum sentence and be released (theoretically) within a few years if he has obeyed all the rules. (I will go more deeply into the criteria for release later in the paper.)

Obeying rules is not as easy as it may sound. In the prison, it's not something left to each man's self-control as much as it is "on the outside." Situations of self-defense arise much more often and an inmate can find himself in serious trouble for defending himself (against homosexual attacks, for example) or protecting his life. For decades it has been observed and ignored that guards provoke violence, racial violence particularly; it is one of their most reliable ways of easily dealing with "problem" inmates, especially minorities—and of the minorities, especially Blacks. The racial walls surrounding each ethnic group are impregnable to all other racial groups. Since this is to the advantage of the guards, who confine "subversive" activity to conspirators of a single group, they promote interracial suspicion and hate whenever they can—as a matter of control tactics. Therefore, interracial arguments, fights and killings are common. Although it is rare for fights to errupt intraracially, it does sometimes happen (informers, for example, are hated by everyone). But it can never be provoked among Blacks by a white guard, and he would seldom try it because it makes his position all too clear to the Blacks, who suspect all guards anyway, and that would eventually endanger the guard's life. It's too big a risk for him, and it's really not necessary because the Black inmate can always expect to be harassed by guard-provoked whites who are rewarded with favors like an easier job in the prison, an overlooked offense, smuggled-in narcotics and other contraband—guards are known to have even smuggled in knives to be used in these attacks—or more special privileges, etc. It is interesting to note that a substantial number of guards are from the south and an overwhelming amount are retired non-commission officers from World War II or retired policemen. *Ramparts* magazine published an expository article in their January 1970 issue, which the reader might wish to refer to entitled "Racism at San Quentin."

I hope I have made clear the fact that Black inmates particularly (although I am using the Correctional Facility at Soledad as my point of reference, it has been long established that prison attitudes and mores differ only slightly with each institution) are harassed by white guards and that physical attacks on them by white inmates are not only sanctioned but sometimes even planned by these guards. When a Black attempts to defend his life, he may be prosecuted for assault; it's the guard's word against his. But it is easy to see how the Black inmate can be manipulated, pressured to the perilous point of retailiation as a result of the social inequities of the prison. The psychological effects of incarceration are next to be discussed.

James V. Bennett, Director of the Bureau of Prisons of the United States Department of Justice, stated recently that "the psychological effect of modern prison life may actually be more brutal than the physical cruelty once commonly practiced in American prisons" . . . and that, "[this statement of conditions] could be applied to almost any American prison." I should like to suggest that the psychological effects Mr. Bennett alludes to are accentuated for the Black man and I intend to clarify and substantiate my suggestion by adding the peculiarities of the Black culture to any analysis of these effects on white inmates done by Gresham Sykes in 1958.

The most apparent effect of imprisonment is the loss of liberty. More psychologically damaging than the spatial restrictions that an inmate suffers is the social severence from family, relatives and friends; not in self-isolation like a hermit but in the involuntary seclusion of the "criminal" . . . They do, of course, have visiting and corresponding privileges but at Soledad, for example, they are limited to ten relatives and/or friends who have to be approved by the institution. Being approved consists of completing an application which will be reviewed by the mail sergeant. The correspondent to an inmate is required to be of a certain age, have no record, if female she must be either unmarried or have her husband sign his approval of the correspondence on the application, and must have known the inmate for at least six years. If an inmate has people who can pass these and other requirements for approval to correspond, he may receive visits and letters and he may write to ten of them. Many inmates have found, however, that their links with the community have been weakened by the time spent behind bars so that a number of their correspondents stop writing and visitation can be nonexistent. (Especially when a man is sent from his home in Los Angeles to prison in Soledad, Folsom or San Quentin; the distance is from 350-450 miles and difficult to make for lower class people particularly.) As a matter of fact, in a random examination of visitation records at the New Jersey State Prison, it was shown that forty-one percent of the inmates had received no visits from the outside world in the past year.[19] This isolation is, of course, painfully depriving and frustrating to all inmates because the loss of emotional relationships, the loneliness, the boredom and the consequent feelings of rejection not only from society but friends: everyone. But it is particularly damaging to the Black inmate. This is the man who has been faced with social rejection for centuries and has found a way to survive with it. Unfortunately, when a man is a social outcast, any substitute means of creating a social structure of his own cannot be expected to conform to that of the society which has rejected him. That is one reason why there are so many Blacks in prison: a conflict between the macro- and sub-cultures as they try to coexist. But once he is there the need to be integrated into some kind of social structure is even more important than before because worse than being slapped (again) with society's rejection, he has been severed from his own subcultural society; temporarily he stands alone. Also, a Black man in prison, where the rules and regulations are numerous, restrictive and clearly defined, is "dichotomized" between belonging to a social complex that incarcerates Blacks and "belonging to" (following the rules of) the prison's code of inmate behavior. Needless to say, there will be circumstances in which the two clash violently, and the Black inmate will have a statement written to the disciplinary board by a guard about his "misconduct." Before he knows it, he may be in trouble again, and the way he got there is completely analogous to the way he got to prison: he is an outcast from society and therefore from its norms.

Another result of imprisonment that Mr. Sykes mentions is the deprivation of goods and services. Before discussing the effect this has on the Black inmate, it is important that we reiterate some of the characteristics of the ghetto environment from which most of them acquire their economic standards so that we may see the special psychological problems they face.

As I have implied before, it is essential to a great portion of lower-class Blacks to "prove" they have money, thereby proving that they *are* someone— as a repudiation to the majority of Americans who have tried (and often successfully) to convince them that they are not. The most expedient proof that the Black man can manage for his peers is to consume as many luxury items as possible (while trying to keep them unaware of the credit problems he is incurring)! On a visit to the ghetto one would undoubtedly notice that the styles of dress are not necessarily comfortable but indispensibly flashy. This is the most common "proof" because it is the most inexpensive. The more ambitious (or perhaps just those with better credit) drive new *large* and expensive cars—the larger the car, the bigger one's image. So it becomes clear that to a man who has always been told he is nothing, having something (expensive items to reflect his worth to himself and his peers) is psychologically essential.

Now, when a man enters prison he is stripped of absolutely everything and all his possessions are kept by the administration until he is released. He is given a set of prison clothes (in California these are called "prison blues"— blue denim trousers and light blue work shirts), prison-made shoes, a pair of socks . . . just the bare necessities to adequately clothe a man and again, these clothes are not his but are just to be used by him. Mr. Sykes sees this as the core of the prisoner's problems in the area of goods and services.

[The prisoner] wants—or needs if you will—not just the so-called necessities of life but also the amenities: cigarettes and liquor as well as calories, interesting foods as well as sheer bulk, individual clothing as well as adequate clothing, individual furnishings for his living quarters as well as shelter, privacy as well as space.[20]

And Mr. Sykes adds, as I have previously stated, that whatever the discomforts and irritations of the inmates' ascetic existence may be, he must carry the additional burden of the social definitions which equate his material deprivation with personal inadequacy. But, according to Mr. Sykes, the white inmate's particular problem is that he identifies more with our money-oriented environment and therefore the failure to "have" is his failure because he did not (could not) "achieve" in his *own* society. The Black man, on the other hand, rather than identifying *with* this society, identifies against it—if you will. [This statement relates primarily to the lower-class man as does the entire paper.] Because the society, as he sees it, has cheated and stolen from him, he feels a certain arrogant pride in being able to retaliate by cheating and stealing from (thereby defying) it. So again, once in the prison he begins to defy its oppression in the same way with the same equally important aims among which recurs the gain of material possessions. It is important to note at least this one major difference between cheating and stealing on the outside and the same behavior on the inside. Unlike conditions on the outside, a Black man's allies and enemies are distinctly defined— by race and rank. A "brother" would never steal from a "brother." The Black "clique" in the institution is a close one and they all trust each other (unless one is thought or proven to be an informer—of "misconduct" to a guard—then he is immediately ostracized and his life may be in jeopardy). *Chicanos* are all right to talk to but not to trust; and whites—well, you could get a bad reputation just talking to one. Needless to say, all guards are "pigs." So usually, in order to ameliorate his Spartan existence with what is available, the Black inmate may either gamble among friends (one could be "reported" for gambling so an inmate chooses carefully with whom he plays) or steal from the enemy; if he can't get it by sheer theft he makes deals, bartering contraband for more contraband all of which are means of attaining what even Mr. Sykes states men need. Black men who blame society for being where they are (as opposed to the white man who blames himself) will habitually react within the psychological framework of the ghetto ethos which directs him to reconstitute his being by acquisition.

A third "pain of imprisonment" that Mr. Sykes mentions is the deprivation of heterosexual relationships. As near as I can tell, sex has always played an important role in the American male's self-esteem, but this is particularly true for the "worthless" minorities. Another minority in this country, the *Chicanos* have even a term—*macho*—which translates loosely to "he-mule" (among other words connoting virility) to identify its men. *Machismo* has many names in the Black man's sphere but the connotations are the same; and it is still "understood" that the more women one has, the more masculine he is. With this concept in mind, we can see that prison creates another difficult problem for the Black inmate. Deprived of heterosexual relationships he is left only with abstention or engagement in homosexual activities. It is unlikely that any man in an institution for a long period of time will be able to abstain for the duration of his stay. Therefore, homosexual relationships are rather common—so common, in fact, that everyone who engages in them is not necessarily considered a homosexual. The problem of sexual frustration is understood and felt by all. It is usually only those who completely and whole-heartedly "turn out" (become homosexual by choice) who are labeled "queens" (known homosexuals). But what is it for a man who places such a high value on masculinity to temporarily engage in sexual deviance prompted by a biological drive? What effect does it have on him? Usually, the conscious guilt feelings of Black inmates are tremendous. Because masculinity is stressed in the ghetto, homosexuality is rare and considered even more "freakish" by this society than it is by the white. (Not that Blacks are biologically immune; Black homosexuals inevitably move away from the ghetto to other, more liberal sections of the city—in Los Angeles they frequently move to Hollywood.) It is adamantly denounced and deplored so that a Black temporary homosexual in the prison realizes the dichotomy of his actions and how detached they are from the ghetto "code" that he constantly lives by.

Besides directly attacking one's manhood and consequently producing guilt complexes, the deprivation of heterosexual relationships deals a striking blow to a man's ego. The inmate is ostracized from the world of women which, by its very polarity, gives the male world much of its meaning. Like most men, the inmate must search for his identity not simply within himself but also in other's reactions to him. Unfortunately, in the prison, only that portion of his personality which is recognized by men has the chance of being appreciated. Again, his image of himself is fractured and distorted.

To be adult enough to be sent to prison but find that once there you are treated like a child is another issue to be faced by inmates. The deprivation of autonomy is another blow at the very foundation of manhood. Mr. Sykes notes,

> *. . . that the frustration of the prisoner's ability to make choices and the frequent refusals to provide explanations for the regulations and commands descending from the bureaucratic staff involve a profound threat to the prisoner's self-image because they reduce the prisoner to the weak, helpless, dependent status of childhood.*

He continues:

> *It is possible that this psychological attack is particularly painful in American culture because of the deep-lying insecurities produced by the delays, the conditionality and the uneven progress so often observed in the granting of adulthood.*[21]

And I should only like to add that to the man who has always been called "boy," this deprivation is particularly excrutiating.

It is established, then, that for the Black man especially, imprisonment is quite painful and includes more injurious consequences than merely the loss of liberty. The significant hurts lie in such additional deprivations as that of autonomy, goods and services, etc. But it is imperative that we realize that these pains provide the incentive and motivation for Black rebellion—that we will examine next.

What is supposed to happen when an inmate is "written up" (a write-up is a written complaint by a guard) is that he is sent to the "disciplinary board" which consists of a varying group of three administrators in the prison (a counselor, for example, or a lieutenent of the guards). The board is supposed to read the officer's account of the inmate's alleged "bad conduct" and (somehow) decide his guilt or innocence, release him back to the cell or punish him with extra work or isolation—something befitting the offense and make a note of the offense in the inmate's record (jacket). Needless to say, it's never worked this way for a Black man (I'm not sure whether it's ever worked quite this way for even whites, but as I'll soon explain, they appear before the board much less often). It is frequently the case that a "troublemaking" inmate will be written up for an offense for which the supervising guard could find no culprit, and it is often that these "troublemakers" are Black. From what I have been told by Black inmates who have been written up, when they go before the board they have no opportunity for a defense; their guilt is assumed. Even if the guard is found to be wrong, the board will excuse itself by saying, "We know you are guilty but we're going to let you go this time; you'd better watch it." Usually he is convicted—of anything from using profanity at a guard or gambling to assault—and must face some kind of punishment. But more harmful to the inmate than the punishment is the write up itself; it becomes a permanent part of his "jacket" to be reviewed by the parole board during his interview for possible release. It is essential to bring the parole board a "clean jacket" (none or few write-ups) for as long a consecutive period as possible before one appears before them. Any write-ups can and usually do affect whether or not the board considers a man sufficiently rehabilitated to re-enter society. Now, because Black men are often written up for crimes they did not commit, and commit many offenses for reasons previously mentioned or more personal ones, it is likely that they will appear before the board with less consecutive "clean time" than many whites and are probably more often denied parole ("shot down"). A recent example of Black men conveniently charged with the stabbing of a guard because the administration considered their Black Power allegiance subversive is "The Soledad 3." With absolutely no evidence against them, these men were chosen to be tried for the death of Officer Schull last summer, but after ten days of trial their case was dismissed for lack of evidence. The only witnesses were some white inmates who later broke down under cross-examination and admitted they lied and were influenced to do so by prison guards. The Soledad 3 were completely innocent but when they appear before the board, there will be an account of the incident in their "jackets," if what I hear from ex-cons about the parole board is true, they, much like the disciplinary board will assume guilt and will give them credit only for beating the rap. This will undoubtedly weight heavily on these men's parole chances. But no inmate is really sure what the Adult Authority (the parole board) wants. James Wagner, one of the Soledad 3, once told me that shortly after Whitney Young's death, some of the questions the board asked Black inmates dealt with how they felt about it. The implications were that if the inmate cared too much about it, he would be considered a militant and not sufficiently rehabilitated to re-enter society. The Adult Authority say they want "clean time", plenty of work, vocational classes that are offered in the prison, church and as much academic education as is offered. I personally know of one inmate who brought them all of this and was "shot down" and cannot reappear for another year.

The difficulty for Blacks in getting a parole date is compounded compared to the difficulty for whites because, as a group, Blacks are frequently victimized. This helps account for the high percentage of Blacks in prison; they are arrested easier and released slower than most whites. But Black men are eventually released. What special problems of resocialization does each have to face?

How Long Can He Stay Out . . . ?

The problems of re-entering society for the ex-con are many and extremely difficult to surmount. He leaves the institution with the expectation not to return; still the rate of recidivism is extremely high and climbing. What happens to the ex-con after the time of release that causes his re-incarceration? What makes the Black man *particularly* so prone to recidivism?

The first problem that the inmate who is approved for release by the parole board must solve is finding some financial support. He *must* have some means of support by the time of his release date and if he fails in doing this his date will probably be delayed until he does. Financial support can mean a relative agreeing to support the returning con; but since most cons come from the lower class, the incidence for this kind of support is quite rare, particularly for the ghetto-based Black families. Often it is left up to the inmate to find a job by correspondence through agencies, family or friends while he is still in the institution. This is quite a formidable task. First of all, most employers are afraid of hiring ex-cons. They seem to be as afraid of their "irresponsibility" as they are of their "tendency toward dishonesty." Second, ex-cons often have no valuable skills. They attend trade classes in the institution as a prerequisite for release but the trades they learn are seldom those in demand. They may learn how to make shoes or some kind of metal craft but they are lost when the job market calls for computer programmers, for example. If the parolee cannot find employment, as is often the case, he may have relatives or friends on the outside set up a "shuck" job for him. This is done by using a friend's name as a fictitious employer and creating a job which seems likely for him. The parolee still has no real means of support, but he has fulfilled the parole board's requirement for release. If the inmate cannot come up with a job (real or fictitious) he leaves it up to his parole agent to find him one. If he can't the inmate will probably be released to an agency for ex-cons which will give him space in a dorm-like house with other ex-cons until he can find employment. If the inmate performs this feat of finding someone who will hire him, it is usually for a job that no one else wants to do, "the hardest and filthiest jobs at 'slave labor.'"[22]

The problem for high-school-educated Black men in finding jobs to keep them even slightly above the level of subsistence is much too difficult. For the Black ex-con, it is virtually impossible; yet he too has to subsist. Let's say he finds a job and a place to stay. He lives either at a friend's or relative's, at the "halfway house" (the agency for parolees), or, as happens all too often, he is alone in a cheap (possibly "skid row") hotel room complete with the dingy grayness and the lingering derelicts so often a part of the scene. One Soledad recidivist described his experience in a place like this:

The parole officer put me in some hotel that had a bunch of winos in the lobby. I had to sneak in the back door because I didn't want anyone to see me walking in the place. This time I'm not gonna let him stick me back in one of those places.[23]

Loneliness is one of the most disturbing problems for the ex-con who ends up in such a place rather than with someone who willingly supports him. He re-enters his home city perhaps expecting the good company of old friends but, as one San Quentin parolee put it, "... all we have in common was the past."[24] Most ex-cons try and stay away from those who they think might lead them to trouble. Having no old friends to comfort him seems on the surface like a problem to be solved by time. But to a con who has been "out of circulation" for a number of years, meeting new people is difficult. First of all, the style of clothes has probably changed since he was last "on the streets" so, in his old clothes he looks strange and out of place. The vernacular has undoubtedly changed so he sounds strange. He has no transportation to social functions and even trying to "pick-up" a girl in a bar is hard. According to a parolee living in Oakland:

I been goin' down to this little bar close to the center. But I ain't got no front. You know man, no car, no clothes. I get into a conversation with some little chick, but she puts me right down. She don't want to look down inside me to see what I got goin'. All these chicks have nice jobs and new cars, nice clothes and big egos. A sucker wearing a joint suit, no apartment, no car ain't got a chance.[25]

So the lonely ex-con easily stays lonely until he becomes equipped mentally and materially to rejoin society. A man who has spent years in "the joint" and is trained to *react* to bells and a P.A. system while being told not to act on his own may have a hard time adjusting to his new "freedoms." He must re-orient himself now that his "boss" has receded so that a glance at a clock might suggest what he can do with his leisure time in place of an ever-present voice directing his actions.

Another problem was probed by *Time* magazine earlier this year in an issue devoted to American penal institutions which dealt with parolees entitled, "Prisons: School for Crime." It is inevitable that when an inmate leaves "the joint," he knows more about how to commit felonies than he's ever known before by listening to other inmates who have committed them for a living. It is quite possible that a man who committed a crime out of necessity and was ready to give up crime when first faced with imprisonment will now think seriously about "pulling a job" using his newly gained knowledge and this time feeling sure he won't be caught.

But I think that by far the most catalyzing situation to probable recidivism for a Black ex-con is that he returns to his home, the ghetto, and is faced with the same "code" of life which led him to prison in the first place. Unlike the white ex-con who has many different parts of town in which to live in social comfort (around other whites) each lower-class Black neighborhood is part of a ghetto. The Black man finds himself torn between "keeping clean" and belonging to his group of "brothers." When he tries to mix the two, and he often does, the tension and frustration mount ... his chances of "making it" are pretty slim.

168

Sometimes not, but too often the Black ex-con winds up a con again. The obstacle course to liberty is too treacherous and tricky for many Blacks. Psychologically and materially defeated as a possible member of the macro culture, his anger and defiance become an integral part of his subculture. And re-entering society is absurd to the man who was never allowed to enter it in the first place. But to the society which catalyzed his contempt, he is only another Black criminal, and he gets just what he deserves.

DEIRDRE'S POEM

Silence
Is Death
It is empty and cold and
Is the antithesis of love.

It does not fight on the side of honest men and women.

Compassion and TRUTH
At the risk of personal loss
Compadres, take your vow
A living vow
One that speaks to Love and Revolution

It is not a question of either or
You live the goodness of your soul
      or
You exist in the sin of a death-filled silence.

If the courts will not affirm the dignity of human kind

    Then we must drag the beasts into the street
    And
    DESTROY THEM
    BY ANY MEANS
    NECESSARY . . .

I watch in horror
As the law follows and condemns those who live in beauty.
But I won't stand by
I will add my name to the list of condemned
The List of Love . . .

In the end,
The victory will be ours . . .
Death's victory is temporary
Others after us
Will pick up the struggle
Where we have fallen.

Deirdre Stone
Cowell College, UCSC

CONCLUSION

Prisoners and students represent, on the surface, the most diametric manifestations of class divisions in American society. Prisons are disproportionately comprised of individuals of color who have grown up in this nation's black urban ghettos and brown barrios. Having been denied the socioeconomic advantages upon which success in America depends, they have fallen victim to a system of justice which accords opportunity and upward mobility only to those who can pay for it, regardless of individual talents and aspirations. Universities, on the other hand, are deliberately designed to support those privileged white, middle and upper-class individuals who, in agreeing to participate in the existing order, provide the single guarantee for its preservation.

But our prisons have become universities of the poor. Both the prisons and universities are basically institutions where human beings are socialized and/or re-socialized. Both attempt to prepare their charges for membership in society per standards and models which are economically determined and implemented by a vast bureaucratic system. Both stress the normative values of the society and each, in its own way, rewards and punishes those assigned to the institution.

The reward for success in the university is to stay within it. The reward for success in the prison is to get out of it. The punishment for failure in the university is to be sent from it. The punishment for failure in the prison is to be constrained within it.

As educators and penologists have learned, it is not always possible to effectively socialize young people according to the dictates of those who are in control of society. Primarily because of technology, neither the prisons nor the universities are in total isolation from the rest of society. So that even as they are pressured and manipulated by the institutional processes of reward and punishment, both inmates and students remain in contact with the development of events taking place in the streets of this nation. Both groups seek to study and synthesize the thoughts and teachings of Karl Marx, Che Guevara, George Jackson, Mao Tse Tung, and others who have forged or are forging the revolutionary parameters of the future. Both of these centers of learning have become places for the speculative investigation of social relationships as they are today and as they could be tomorrow. And for those who do not fear intellectual freedom and creative thought, this struggling search by students and prisoners for a key to a freer world is certainly exciting and, above all else, reassuring.

There are some individuals within the penal and education professions who willingly acknowledge the failure of the system and who seek, if not radical or utopian alternatives, at least humane changes within the existing structures. The Soledad administrators who gave support to our class must be counted among these. Surely they had to compromise apprehensions at the prospect of allowing a racially-mixed group of both male and female college students to enter the uneasy climate of Soledad prison. It has become a foregone conclusion in the minds of prison authorities that sustained involvement between prisoners and outsiders will have a disruptive potential in the life of the prison. Representatives of the California State Board of Corrections have repeatedly blamed the recent history of turmoil within the state prisons on radical outside influences. It is of course a classic guilt reaction on the part of those who are guarding injustice to look beyond themselves in assigning blame for protests and unrest among those supposedly under their control. To believe that prisoners are incapable of recognizing on their own the unjust and inhuman processes of the American penal and judicial systems is to be foolishly blind. To lay the blame for insurgencies within prisons on "outside agitators" is analogous to the charge that "student unrest" is similarly a response to outside agitation. Prisoners and students are protesting against their respective institutions because they, better than anyone, know how and to what destructive ends their individual and collective lives are being manipulated by the institutions and by the society which creates and supports them.

It is becoming virtually impossible to totally cut off either the universities or the prisons from the society which surrounds them. Both students and prisoners have begun to seriously understand and articulate the contradictions and failures of that society. Classes comprised of both university students and prison inmates serve the mutually beneficial function of giving students contact with experiences which make their abstract theoretical undertakings real, and providing prisoners with an intellectual context through which they can better define the reality of their lives. Such was the experience of Politics 190C: Utopian Studies. Through their interchange, students and prisoners alike were aroused to a careful and reasoned examination of the world as it is and of the possibilities that we must grasp in forming the world's future. Although the course was designed with a conventional academic format, the group discussions led to a sharing of very personal experiences and attitudes, which could then be positioned within a broad social context and analysis. Thus, the class gave human content to academic abstractions and meaningful form to the enforced monotony of prison life.

It is both pragmatically necessary and morally correct for us to demand that our institutions facilitate communication between those who are confined within our prison walls and those whose task as students it is to analyze and eventually educate the society which constructs those walls. Certainly a striking lesson learned by all of us in the class is that education is not something you can get within university walls any more than rehabilitation is something you can get in a cage.

Implicit in the preceding pages is a plea to foreclose our existing penal system. This is not to dismiss the very real and tragic fact that within our prisons there are men and women who have inflicted severe and often irreparable damage on innocent persons. (Certainly there are many more such dangerous or irresponsible persons outside our prisons than within, but whose privileged position in the society ensures the maintenance of their own extra-legal system of justice.) And as long as our society continues in its failure to correctly understand and respond to the human needs of all its members, such deviancy will be guaranteed and forms of social control will remain necessary. The common approach to rising crime rates has been to expand our police forces and to attempt reform within our correctional institutions. But efforts to provide more effective and more humane methods of social control through penal reforms have been in no way successful. Prisons most blatantly represent the economic class divisions inherent in a capitalist society. Third World people, through the institutionalized processes of racism, are delegated to the lowest economic positions. And it is most often poor people who go to prison. A person from a ghetto, whether innocent or guilty, is far more likely to be arrested than is her or his white middle or upper-class counterpart. A poor person cannot afford to make bail, cannot hire competent defense attorneys, and cannot rely on the influence of establishment connections to avoid conviction and imprisonment. Thus, while Third World persons account for only 16% of the California population, 45% of the state prison population is black and brown. Even apart from the factor of *whom* we imprison, it is important to recognize that our prisons fail to do for us that which we expect them to do, and that it is as impractical as it is immoral to maintain our existing institutions. As evidenced in the recidivism rates and post-prison histories of convicted offenders, there is no positive correlation between the penalties for crime and the deterrance and/or prevention of crime. Prisons arouse contempt rather than respect for our judicial system. Prisons do not rehabilitate; rather they develop a criminal class from among those who are subjected to them. Prisons offer panaceas to those who believe that our streets are safer with the bad guys locked up, a logic wholly ignoring the reality that less than 50% of our crimes are ever resolved and a "resolved" crime does not insure that the convicted individual did in fact commit that crime. Prisons offer no redeeming social value. Prisons create more crimes than they prevent and the problem of prisons cannot be constructively understood or dealt with until we begin concentrating on all those socio-economic factors which make prisons necessary.

In comparing our respective worlds, both students and prisoners came to see the inherent flaws of the greater society which developed into the anti-human aspects of both institutions. Prisons and universities, no matter how strictly isolated from the rest of the society, are still reflections of the authoritarianism, racism and social mystification of the greater institution—the society at large. It is relatively easy to point out the inhuman and anti-human aspects of the prison system. But in order to effectively change the concepts which allow such institutions to arise within a culture, in order to effectively understand and confront the economic power structure which is fundamental to that culture, it is necessary to view all cultural institutions in the same analytical terms. This condition is essential if we are to make any positive changes in the social consciousness toward prisons and thereby affect serious changes from within the prisons themselves.

Karlene Faith
Ralph Guzman
Santa Cruz, 1972

REFERENCES

[1] Selin, Thorsten. "Paley on the Time Sentence," *Journal of the American Institute of Criminal Law and Criminology,* 1922, Vol. 22, p. 264.

[2] Lindsey, Edward. "Historical Sketch of the Indeterminate Sentence and Parole System," *Journal of the American Institute of Criminal Law and Criminology,* 1926, Vol. 16, p. 16.

[3] Hayner, Norman S. "Sentencing by an Administrative Board," *Law and Contemporary Problems,* 1968, Vol. 23, p. 489.

[4] Hoebel, E. A. *The Cheyennes,* p. 51.

[5] *Ibid.*

[6] Farb, Peter. *Man's Rise to Civilization,* p. 84.

[7] Graham, Fred P. "Black Crime," *Harper's Magazine,* September 1970.

[8] Updike, John. "Black Suicide," *Atlantic Magazine,* February 1971.

[9] Graham, *op. cit.*

[10] Anonymous, "Education," *Time Magazine,* April 6, 1970.

[11] *Ibid.*

[12] *Ibid.*

[13] Graham, *op. cit.*

[14] Anonymous, "Law," *Time Magazine,* April 6, 1970.

[15] Anonymous, "Law," *Time Magazine,* April 6, 1970.

[16] Graham, *op. cit.*

[17] Updike, *op. cit.*

[18] "Law," *Time, op. cit.*

[19] Sykes, Gresham M. *The Society of Captives.* 1958, p. 65.

[20] *Ibid.,* p. 68.

[21] *Ibid.,* pp. 75-76.

[22] Irwin, John. *The Felon.* 1970.

[23] *Ibid.,* p. 123.

[24] *Ibid.,* p. 132.

[25] *Ibid.,* p. 140.

in 5/2 PK